EU Federalism and Constitutionalism

EU Federalism and Constitutionalism

The Legacy of Altiero Spinelli

Edited by
Andrew Glencross and
Alexander H. Trechsel

LEXINGTON BOOKS

A division of
ROWMAN & LITTLEFIELD PUBLISHERS, INC.
Lanham • Boulder • New York • Toronto • Plymouth, UK

Published by Lexington Books
A division of Rowman & Littlefield Publishers, Inc.
A wholly owned subsidiary of The Rowman & Littlefield Publishing Group, Inc.
4501 Forbes Boulevard, Suite 200, Lanham, Maryland 20706
www.lexingtonbooks.com

Estover Road, Plymouth PL6 7PY, United Kingdom

British Library Cataloguing in Publication Information Available

Library of Congress Cataloging-in-Publication Data

EU federalism and constitutionalism : the legacy of Altiero Spinelli / edited by Andrew Glencross and Alexander H. Trechsel.
p. cm.
Includes bibliographical references and index.
ISBN 978-0-7391-3334-7 (cloth : alk. paper) — ISBN 978-0-7391-3335-4 (electronic)
1. European Union. 2. Constitutional history—European Union countries. 3. Federal government—European Union countries. 4. Spinelli, Altiero. 5. European federation. I. Glencross, Andrew. II. Trechsel, Alexandre H. III. Title: European Union federalism and constitutionalism.
JN30.E81952 2010
341.242'2—dc22 2010030539

∞™ The paper used in this publication meets the minimum requirements of American National Standard for Information Sciences—Permanence of Paper for Printed Library Materials, ANSI/NISO Z39.48-1992.

Printed in the United States of America

Contents

List of Tables

Foreword

I think that not only scholars and students of European Union affairs but also active citizens and politicians could learn about the past of European integration and inform themselves about its future if they take the time to read the contributions written by the authors of this volume. The Treaty of Lisbon entered into force on 1 December 2009, thereby concluding a very long period of intergovernmental bargaining concerning the reform of the 1957 treaties of Rome, to allow:

a. the realization of the essential aims set out in the founding treaties and mainly to perfect the internal market.
b. the efficiency and the democratic nature of the institutional system in a community gradually increased from six to twenty-seven member countries and more in the near future.
c. the attribution to the European Union of new competencies in fields having a clear European dimension.

Encouraged by the Spinelli Treaty, the European "building site" has been in operation from June 1985 (European Council in Milan) to December 2009 (entry into force of the Treaty of Lisbon). To summarize the six stages of the reform:

- the *Single European Act*—the first overall modification of the treaties—entered into force in 1987 but the governments reopened the debate in

1988 to mark a second stage of the reform and achieve Economic and Monetary Union after the Internal Market

- the *Treaty of Maastricht*, negotiated between December 1990 and December 1991, entered into force in 1993 but the governments reopened the debate in 1995 to mark a third stage of the reform and reach the "Ioannina compromise" in view of the enlargement of the European Union
- the *Treaty of Amsterdam*, negotiated between February 1996 and June 1997, entered into force in 1999 but the governments immediately reopened the debate to reach a fourth stage of the reform and finish business left over from the Treaty of Amsterdam
- the *Treaty of Nice*, negotiated between December 1999 and December 2000, entered into force in 2003 but the governments reopened the debate in 2001 to mark the fifth stage of the reform and constitutionalize the EU institutional system.
- the *Constitutional Treaty*, negotiated between February 2002 (first meeting of the European Convention) and June 2004 (end of the Inter Governmental Conference) never entered into force because of the negative results of the referendums in France and the Netherlands and the decision of the 2007 German presidency to consign it to the archives.
- the *Lisbon Treaty*, negotiated between January and June 2007 and a subsequent IGC from July and October 2007, was signed in Lisbon on 13 December 2007. It entered into force on 1 December 2009.

The Lisbon Treaty brings important changes to the existing treaties. It will make the European Union more democratic, transparent (1), and effective (2) and it will lead to a Union of enhanced rights, values, solidarity, and security (3). It will improve the visibility and capacity of the Union to act on the global stage (4) and so will give it the tools to deliver on citizens' expectations.

The new Treaty introduces a more democratic and transparent Europe with a strengthened role for the European and national parliaments, greater openness in the decision-making process, more opportunities for citizens to intervene and a clearer sense of who does what at the European and national levels. The new Treaty will make the European Union more effective, with reformed institutions that work in a Union of twenty-seven (and more) member states, with quicker decision making, an improved ability in areas of major priorities for today's Union and simplified and fairer voting rules. The new Treaty will establish a Europe of rights and values, solidarity and security with a clear focus on the Union's values and objectives. The new Treaty will give equal legal and political standing to the rules established by and in the Treaty and the rights established by and in the Charter of Nice.

The new Treaty will also strengthen the European Union as an actor on the global stage by bringing together Europe's external policy tools, both in policy development and policy delivery. It will give Europe a clear voice in relations with partners worldwide; bring more coherence between the different strands of EU external policy, and harness Europe's economic, political and diplomatic strengths to promote European interests and values worldwide.

Unless there is a serious institutional crisis, the European "building site" will be idle for a long time. After the institutional reforms, the future European debate will be devoted to policies to establish the nature of the European Union in view of 2020. National and European institutions should clearly explain to the citizens what is now "our Fundamental Law" (the Treaty of Lisbon), how the institutional system works and what is the actual relationship between the European Union and its member states.

The last rehash of the reform seems however a very modest compromise in an objective comparison with the ambitions of the Laeken Declaration and the first debates in the European Convention. The Treaty of Lisbon has to be judged as a starting point for a new constitutional debate in the distant future. Nevertheless, the innovations made in the treaties will have a great influence on the daily work of the institutions and on the perception of the citizens.

As Paolo Ponzano writes in his contribution, a great number of the innovations introduced by the Lisbon Treaty are inspired by the text adopted by the European Parliament in 1989 even if some elements were not incorporated in the treaty or disappeared during the journey from the Convention to the last IGC.

It is well known that Spinelli made federation the starting point of the unification process in Europe. In the face of the defeats of his actions, from the decision taken by the governments to rebuild their national sovereignty after the Second World War to the rebuff of his Draft Treaty in 1985, Spinelli maintained his idea that unification can only be achieved by a unitary power. From his point of view, the most important result of European integration is not the list of what Jean Monnet called "concrete achievements"—because they are modest and precarious when compared to the new and growing challenges to Europe in the world—or the false idea that a European administration will prevail against the national governments. Finally when one analyzes objectively the progress of European integration, the most important thing has been the transformation in political consciousness, which obliges us to preserve what has been built and prompts us to continue to view our main problems in European terms, despite the mediocrity of our achievements and the long list of opportunities missed, wasted or sabotaged.

Contrary to what many scholars and politicians say, the history of European integration showed that it was the "*méthode de l'engrenage*" (incremental change) invented by Jean Monnet that failed and not the principles of a European constitutionalism fostered by Altiero Spinelli and his associates.

If the intergovernmental or communitarian method, when systematically employed, provided Europeans with an efficient government or with an efficient multilevel governance able to cope with their common interests, it could be said that—although it is oligarchic and bureaucratic since power is exercised by a handful of ministers and senior officials—it does at least deal with the problems effectively, promptly, correctly, and with continuity.

But the fact is that in the crucial fields of external and security policy on the one hand and of economic policy on the other hand, the process of taking decisions through councils or European Councils is by nature inefficient, slow, unsatisfactory and offers no guarantee of continuity.

The recent experience of the financial crisis and the European response (or the lack of European response) showed that this procedure has the effect of "loading the dice": everything of national interest emerges as a priority, everything of truly European interest remains submerged and is relegated to a minor position.

All the contributions written for this volume show that—as Andrew Glencross suggests—the constitutional dialogue is far from over and that we have to go "back to the future" based on the federalist principles elaborated by Altiero Spinelli.

Pier-Virgilio Dastoli
Former personal assistant to Altiero Spinelli

Acknowledgments

The progenitor of this volume was the conference "From Spinelli to the Reform Treaty: Ideas, Successes, and Failures of European Federalism and Constitutionalism," hosted at the European University Institute, Florence, on October 12, 2007. We are grateful to all the participants who attended this conference, skillfully organized as ever by Gabriella Unger, as well as to Professor Yves Mény who gave the welcome speech.

Andrew Glencross would like to recognize the institutional support of the International Relations Program at the University of Pennsylvania. His contribution, "Altiero Spinelli and the Idea of the U.S. Constitution as a Model for Europe" originally appeared in 2009 in *JCMS: The Journal of Common Market Studies* 47 (3): 287–307, and is reproduced here with permission. He would also like to thank Jonathan de Jong and Laura White for their exceptionally diligent editorial assistance on the manuscript.

Introduction

Spinelli's Heritage: An Introduction to the European Union's Post-Lisbon Challenge

Alexander H. Trechsel

With the ratification of the Treaty of Lisbon in 2009 and its subsequent entry into force, the European Union has given itself a long-needed institutional structure that corresponds better, at first sight, to its contemporary and future needs. Although the treaty abandoned the rhetoric of a constitution, it nonetheless reprised the vast majority of the changes originally present in the defunct Constitutional Treaty. It took heads of state across the EU two years, following the two negative referendums in France and in the Netherlands, to finally sign the new Treaty in 2007. This same year also marked the centenary of the birth of the most prominent advocate of a federal Europe, Altiero Spinelli, author of the *Ventotene Manifesto*, former European Commissioner and Member of the European Parliament, who persuaded his fellow parliamentarians to adopt the 1984 Draft Treaty on European Union. This volume pays tribute to Altiero Spinelli, producer of indelible imprints on the evolution of Europe.

Today, the European Union faces a profound economic crisis. Member states have had to be bailed out, multibillion dollar funds are created and new instruments for saving the common currency are proposed. With the newly adopted mechanisms introduced by the European Central Bank, the European Commission and the International Monetary Fund, the European Union took an immense step in the direction of a common economic and financial policy. The Commission went as far as proposing a mechanism through which it could get involved in the budgetary process of member states, right at the beginning and before national parliaments get a chance to discuss their respective budget plans. One could argue that the European Union has reached a watershed, where it either fully federalizes its structures or has to face the risk of dismantlement. The crisis opens up one Pandora's box after the other. Member states openly discuss the limits of their solidarity with each other. Non-Eurozone member states question whether they should contribute to solving the Euro's problems. At the same time, national governments start questioning the constitutionality of the proposed measures: do they go too far and breach the terms set by the Lisbon Treaty? Are the mechanisms set in place by the new Treaty antiquated before they can deploy their effects? Does yet another round of treaty change become unavoidable? And if so, can it be done despite the looming referendum threats at the member state level?

One of the finest experts in the field of federalism, the late William Riker, argued that federations were born out of necessity, that is, when states face a military threat. According to Riker, only if there was a reason for aggregating resources could such a federalization process become a reality. And military motives remain, for Riker, the main reason for aggregating resources, with trade motives remaining secondary. In the case of the European Union he conceded that the economic motive may eventually trump the military one. Overall however, he remained skeptical about such prospects.[1] The situation facing the European Union since the economic crisis hit the world in 2008 to 2009 requires a rethinking of Riker's skepticism. On the one hand, Europe needs to uphold its internal market. It cannot afford states such as Greece or Portugal, and even less so Spain, to go bankrupt. Even if these member states could be "sacrificed," the Euro would possibly crumble and bring the entire continent, including non-Eurozone member states, to its knees. Add to this the political impossibility of allowing such cataclysmic events to happen. One may soundly hypothesize that in the case of nonaction, not only the Euro, but the European Union may crumble. In other words, the European Union is obliged to give itself the necessary powers to prevent such scenarios from becoming reality. Rapid and profound federalization of economic and financial policies and of the mechanisms determining the latter may well become the only alternative to a process of dismantling the quasi-federal structure the European Union has already acquired. More than possibly ever before, the institutional and political options for a European Federation must be considered carefully. In this sense, by looking back, at the ideas of Altiero Spinelli, this volume also looks ahead, toward a possible future of the European Union.

This book is the fruit of an international conference convened by the European Union Democracy Observatory (EUDO) of the European University Institute in Florence, in 2007. It focused on Spinelli's federalist and constitutional ideas in the context of European integration, from its origins to the Lisbon Treaty and beyond. The conference brought together an interdisciplinary panel of European scholars from law, history and political science as well as former colleagues of Spinelli from the European Commission. The present volume focuses on the central twofold question of what have been the successes and failures of the establishment of a federally organized Europe and how these relate to Spinelli's own federal vision. The papers presented in the conference have consequently been revised to take account of this overarching theme as well as to include as much discussion as possible of the Lisbon Treaty.

This volume is based on interdisciplinary scholarship that covers all three dimensions of the European project: historical, legal and political. We have structured the book into three sections reflecting, however, different intellectual strategies for assessing the successes and failures of European federalism. The first examines the federalism *problématique* through a constitutional lens; the second adopts a comparative approach to contrast European integration with the development of U.S. federalism; the third and final section studies in detail the treaty-revising process from the perspective of actors and institutions.

Hence part I of the present volume addresses the question of the constitutionalization of European integration. It does so in a twofold manner by revisiting, on the one hand, the development of successive treaty revisions and the jurisprudence of the European Court of Justice and, on the other hand, the 1984 Draft Treaty on European Union, Spinelli's brainchild. In the first chapter, Paolo Ponzano discusses the 1984 Draft Treaty. He does so by demonstrating the far-sightedness of Spinelli's project, which is shown to have begun the process of constitutionalizing the treaties and launching a constitutional debate on the future of integration. Thus, by comparing the 1984 Draft with successive treaty revisions, including the current Lisbon Treaty, the analysis reveals the enormous extent to which Spinelli's innovative proposals have either been incorporated into treaty change or continue to set the terms of debate for reform. In this way, although Spinelli lost the immediate battle for creating a federal, constitutional union, his ideas are shown to continue providing the impetus for trying to solve the institutional challenges facing the EU.

In chapter 2, Stefano Bartolini discusses the concepts of constitutionalism and legitimacy in the context of European integration. He argues that the EU Treaties are not solidly crafted around the fundamental principles of constitutionalism, themselves the fruit of the European enlightenment. The author demonstrates that the discourse concerning the Brussels-generated discourse on the EU's constitution, democracy, legitimacy, etc., is misleading at best. The conceptual mist in which the EU navigates obscures numerous reefs and shallows and increases the risk of wreckage. By further nourishing such misconceptions the EU increases its distance from national electorates and thus commits a "policy mistake" that goes well beyond the theoretical and conceptual mistake unveiled by Bartolini.

Part II of this volume contains two comparisons between the U.S. experience and its European counterpart. In chapter 3, Sergio Fabbrini offers a comparison of the respective origins of the United States of America and the European Union. These two cases were compared by Spinelli already in 1957. However, as Fabbrini argues, the comparative view of Spinelli needs to be redefined: the European construction is not simply mirroring the genesis of the United States. Though both systems have overcome the problem of asymmetry (in terms of their constituent units) by creating horizontal and vertical forms of separation of powers, they are not identical, neither in their constitutional fundamentals nor in their trajectory since their creation. However, they are "compound democracies," characterized by this particular constitutional pluralism induced by the separation-of-power schemes. Comparing these two cases in terms of compound democracies is thus extremely fruitful for a better understanding of the current constitutional momentum the EU has gained, the tensions surrounding this critical juncture and the possible solutions to the problems the latter is facing.

Andrew Glencross, in chapter 4, elaborates on the comparison between the United States and the European Union, by further scrutinizing Spinelli's claim that European integration needs to draw inspiration from the U.S. constitutional founding. It does so in order to compare the predicament of European integration with U.S. constitutional politics. Hence the analysis contrasts how Europe and the United States experienced problems of sovereignty clashes and institutionalizing democratic accountability across the dual separation of powers. It reveals both how Spinelli exaggerated the extent to which the U.S. Constitution established and delimited federal political authority once and for all as well the way in which, despite its functionalist nonconstitutional origins, the EU has developed its own brand of constitutional politics. The comparison thus shows how both polities faced a similar tension between the process of constitutionalism, restraining unit sovereignty, and the institutionalization of popular sovereignty at the federal level.

Having used both a constitutional and comparative lens to view EU federalism and constitutionalism, part III focuses on the actors and institutions engaged in the nexus of treaty revision. In addition, the chapters also discuss the consequences this process has for these same participants. This entails an in-depth study of the design and functioning of the institutional architecture of the EU and its antecedents from Spinelli's Draft Treaty to the Lisbon Treaty. In addition, given that the latter reprises many elements of the former, the volume concludes with an analysis of the fate of Spinelli's Treaty, which had originally attracted the support of then French president François Mitterrand.

Chapter 5, authored by Bruno de Witte, offers a legal analysis of the constitutional politics of treaty architecture in the course of the integration process. In particular, the analysis focuses on the fragmented nature of the treaty system that has existed since the initial postwar moves toward European unity. This approach reveals the legal uncertainties arising from this structure, which the Constitutional Treaty was explicitly intended to address. In this way, the Lisbon Treaty, which returns the EU to a two-treaty system but with the addition of the Charter of Fundamental Rights, is a deliberate political response to the hostility the Constitutional Treaty faced when subjected to referendums. Yet this response will have profound implications for constitutional clarity and thus the effective functioning of the EU.

Jean-Marie Palayret's contribution, contained in chapter 7, explains the fate of the 1984 Draft Treaty promoted by Spinelli and the European Parliament but whose destiny in reality lay in the hands of then French president François Mitterrand. The chapter shows how the latter sought a European policy success, for both domestic and international reasons. Yet despite his original support for Spinelli's endeavor, Mitterrand changed tactics in the face of German ambivalence and British hostility. The result was that Mitterrand seized upon the Dooge Report of 1985 in order to promote institutional reform linked to the completion of the single market. However, this change of direction failed to invalidate the constitutional concerns first raised in the Spinelli Draft Treaty.

In the concluding chapter, Andrew Glencross makes the case for why Spinelli's ideas are likely to continue to contribute greatly to the debate over the future evolution of the EU. The analysis focuses on the constitutional discourse that emerged since the Convention on the Future of Europe and the subsequent Constitutional Treaty. In this context, the Lisbon Treaty is shown to have failed to satisfy certain fundamental expectations for further constitutionalizing the EU. Hence the chapter concludes with a discussion of the options for further federal and constitutional reform inspired by Spinelli's work and the nature of the opposition these are likely to face.

The wide-ranging and analytical scope of this volume clearly goes beyond a narrow "homage" to Spinelli. It not only revives his ideas and discusses them in the light of the events that took place over the course of the European integration process since he wrote his famous "Draft Treaty on European Union." It also shows the richness of Spinelli's ideas for the future of the European Union. While in Spinelli's day European governments could refrain from fully federalizing their Union, by sticking to the unanimity principle for Treaty change, the "muddling through," somewhere between a clear commitment to a federal Union and pure intergovernmentalism, becomes ever more difficult. Should the EU be forced to make clearer choices regarding its own structure and functioning, our discussion of Spinelli's ideas may well contribute practically to this debate.

Note

1. William H. Riker, *Federalism: Origin, Operation, Maintenance* (Boston: Little-Brown, 1964).

PART ONE

THE CONSTITUTIONAL DIMENSION

CHAPTER ONE

The "Spinelli Treaty" of February 1984

The Start of the Process of Constitutionalizing the EU

Paolo Ponzano

On 14 February 1984, at the instigation of Altiero Spinelli, the European Parliament approved a draft treaty as the start of the process of constitutionalizing the European Economic Community. This initiative led first to the revision of the treaties establishing the European Community (the Single European Act, the Treaties of Maastricht, Amsterdam, and Nice) and later to the Constitutional Treaty of 29 October 2004.

Altiero Spinelli made his constitutional attempt—to provide the European Economic Community with a kind of constitutional text—at a time when the European Economic Community was embroiled in negotiations about the amount of Britain's contribution to the European budget, reforming the common agricultural policy and increasing the resources of the Community itself (not to mention negotiations on Spanish and Portuguese accession). In fact, these were the same problems that gripped the European Union in 2005 during the difficult discussions on the financial perspectives for the years 2007 to 2013.

In 1980, the European Parliament was frustrated by the fact that, despite being elected by direct universal suffrage, it did not have real political influence in the European decision-making process (with the sole and essentially negative exceptions of the power to reject the budget adopted by the Council and the power to censure the Commission, but without being able to influence its investiture). Departing from his purely advisory role, Altiero Spinelli decided to prompt the European Parliament to become the "main weapon" of the constituent process within the European Economic Community and to revive the dynamics that were at least supposed to result in the radical reform of the European institutions as conceived by the 1957 Treaties of Rome, if not in the immediate adoption of a European "Constitution." In other words, he decided to take the initiative to lend new impetus to the process of European integration through the drawing-up of a "new Treaty" rather than a simple change of detail in the existing Treaties.

The Spinelli Project

Rereading the draft approved by the European Parliament in February 1984 under the decisive influence of Altiero Spinelli allows us to rediscover its extraordinary relevance and, at the same time, its precursory influence on the subsequent amendments to the Treaties of Rome. The relevance of the Spinelli Project lies at once in the method of drafting the Treaty and in the content of many of its provisions.

In the early 1980s, not unlike the situation today, the process of European integration found itself stuck in discussions about Britain's financial contribution, agricultural policy reform and increasing the Community's own resources. Moreover, the European Economic Community was starting its third expansion to embrace Spain and Portugal without making a provision meanwhile to reinforce its institutional mechanisms and powers. On the other hand, the European Parliament had been elected by direct universal suffrage in 1979 even though its essentially advisory powers remained unaltered. The exception to this rule was the power to reject the budget, which had proved to be a blunt weapon since the Council had been able to adopt a new budget similar to the one rejected by Parliament. The European Parliament's power of censorship over the college of Commissioners was equally blunt since, in the event of a vote of censure, the Member States could simply appoint a college of Commissioners not necessarily as welcoming to the European Parliament as the former (given that, unlike today, the Parliament did not have the power to approve the nomination of the new Commission). Therefore, the European Parliament was in danger of becoming, as Spinelli put it, "an assembly vested with acute moral and political responsibilities but devoid of the competences necessary to exercise them." Like any good strategist, Altiero Spinelli made himself the commentator of this unsatisfactory situation and in a speech to the European Parliament in 1980 he launched a political initiative to give the European Economic Community new powers and to its institutions the means of exercising them. It was in that very speech on 25 June 1980, that Altiero

Spinelli urged the European Parliament to take charge of the future destiny of the European Economic Community and launch the initiative of undertaking a "comprehensive reform" of the Rome Treaties.

In the interest of brevity, I shall confine myself to going over the main stages of Altiero Spinelli's initiative:

a. The creation of the "Crocodile Club" as a cross-party group of innovative European Parliamentarians (reminiscent of the ground-breaking coalition between innovators and conservatives already present in the *Ventotene Manifesto*);
b. The creation of an "Ad Hoc Commission" within the European Parliament in charge of drawing up the draft of the Treaty;
c. Bringing pressure to bear on such prominent political personalities as Enrico Berlinguer, Willy Brandt, Leo Tindemans and finally, after the vote of the European Parliament, François Mitterrand, who Spinelli felt was the political personality most likely to support the Treaty both as the president of France and because of his personal leanings. Spinelli's strategy came to fruition when Mitterrand delivered his speech on 24 May 1984 in Strasbourg: "Expressing myself in the name of France, I declare her ready to examine your proposal, whose spirit it finds most fitting."

Rereading it today, Mitterrand's declaration can be interpreted in the light of other factors, as behind the statement by the president there was also a French interest in supporting the Spinelli Project, as was revealed by J.-M. Palayret, who consulted the French diplomatic archives of the time. This interest lay in using a more ambitious European Union project to counterbalance English minimalism and keep open the option of a two-speed Europe (or one of variable geometry), as Article 82 of the Spinelli Project suggested (once there was a majority of States representing two-thirds of the population, it provided for governments to decide, by common accord, the date on which the Treaty entered into force and the relations with States that had not ratified it). As we can see, this clause is more ambitious than declaration No. 30 attached to the Constitutional Treaty of 29 October 2004, even though it is driven by the same desire to "sidestep" the unanimity rule.

The Essential Elements of the Spinelli Project

Rereading the text of the Treaty of 14 February 1984 shows that most of its innovative provisions were included in successive Treaties or in the text of the Constitutional Treaty of 29 October 2004. Let us go over them briefly.

The Method Used by Spinelli

Altiero Spinelli was the first to argue that a Constitutional Treaty could not be drafted by an intergovernmental conference according to the traditional diplomatic method. Governments adopted this position when, after the Treaty of Nice, they entrusted a European Convention on the Future of Europe with the task of preparing a new draft treaty. Furthermore, in the Spinelli Project there was the germ of participation by national parliaments and civil society, such as emerged later in the European Convention and its methods of work.

The General Structure of the Treaty

The Spinelli Project was intended to be a new institutional Treaty of the European Union and not a mere revision of existing Treaties (unlike the Single European Act, the Treaties of Maastricht, Amsterdam and Nice, but like the Constitutional Treaty of 2004). Therefore, rather than merely amending existing treaties, Altiero Spinelli really started the "constitutional" process of the Union.

Superseding the Various Forms of Political Cooperation/Integration

Article 1 of the Spinelli Project provides for the creation of a European Union that goes beyond the three European Communities that existed in 1984, the European monetary system and political cooperation. It is thus an approach that is equivalent to suppressing the three pillars as provided for by the Constitutional Treaty of 2004 (a suppression that will be maintained by the Lisbon Treaty, which came out of the Intergovernmental Conference that followed the referendum rejections in France and the Netherlands).

European Citizenship

Article 3 of the Spinelli Project introduces the concept of Union citizenship in parallel with national citizenship, the two being closely connected. This concept was revived by the Maastricht Treaty on the European Union (1992) and maintained in successive Treaties.

Fundamental Rights

Article 4 of the Spinelli Project introduced the idea of the fundamental rights that derive from the common principles of the national constitutions, as well as from the European Convention for the Protection of Human Rights and Fundamental Freedoms. This article referred not only to the classic rights of the ECPHR, but also to the new economic and social rights guaranteed by national constitutions—as would be done later by the

Charter of Fundamental Rights promulgated in Nice in 2000 and integrated into the Constitutional Treaty of 2004 as well as the Lisbon Treaty of 2007.

Sanctions Against Member States

To guarantee that fundamental rights are respected, Article 4(4) of the Spinelli Project introduced the principle of penalties against States that are in breach of the democratic principles or the fundamental rights themselves. This provision anticipates the articles later introduced in the Amsterdam Treaty (1996) as well as the subsequent penalties bilaterally applied against Austria by certain Member States in 2000 after the formation of a coalition government that included Joerg Haider's hard-right Freedom party.

The Institutionalization of the European Council

Article 8 of the Spinelli Project introduced the European Council as one of the formal institutions of the Union for the first time (whereas the Treaties of Rome make no mention of it and successive Treaties entrust the European Council with a few functions, but without making it an Institution of the Union). It would take the Constitutional Treaty of 29 October 2004 to "institutionalize" the European Council. In this area, too, the Spinelli Project proved to be the precursor of future constitutional developments.

The Methods of Operation of the Union

Article 10 of the Spinelli Project provided for two methods of operation of the Union. On the one hand, it outlined common action in accordance with the classic Community method (Commission proposal, majority vote of the Council, co-decision of the European Parliament); on the other hand, cooperation between the Member States in accordance with the intergovernmental method. The innovative element of the Spinelli Project is that the Union could move from intergovernmental action to the Community method by decision of the European Council (see Article 11). This provision anticipates the so-called bridging clauses introduced in successive treaties to permit the passage from one decision-making procedure to another more in keeping with the Community method.

The Principle of Subsidiarity

Article 12 of the Spinelli Project introduced the idea for the first time that, in the area of concurrent powers, Union action is necessary if it proves to be more effective than the action of the Member States, particularly when the dimensions of the action of the Union or its effects extend beyond national frontiers. It is the first clear definition of the so-called principle of subsidiarity that would later be introduced into European law by the Maastricht Treaty.

Legislative Co-Decision between the European Council and the European Parliament

The Spinelli Project introduced the concept of a *European law* (taken up again by the Constitutional Treaty of 2004) voted on by the two branches of the legislative body (the European Parliament and the Council). Under this proposal, European law would be adopted by a procedure of co-decision between the European Parliament and the Council, as later provided for by the Maastricht Treaty (except that the European Parliament votes first and the Council then pronounces on the text of Parliament, and not vice versa as in the current system). This difference is explained by the desire to give precedence to the Lower House—the European Parliament—directly elected by the citizens, rather than to the Council of Ministers. The Spinelli Project also made a provision for a *Consultation Committee* between Parliament and Council, with the participation of the Commission, as introduced subsequently by the Maastricht Treaty (based on the German model of the Conciliation Commission between the *Bundestag* and the *Bundesrat*).

The Investiture of the European Commission

The Spinelli Project provided for the European Commission to take up office after obtaining a vote of investiture by the European Parliament. This provision was also included and improved upon in subsequent Treaties.

The Council of the Union

Article 20 of the Spinelli Project provided that the Council of the Union should consist of Ministers who are specifically and permanently responsible for European issues. This provision is a forerunner to the legislative Council provided for in the draft Treaty of the European Convention, although this was not resurrected in the Constitutional Treaty of 2004.

The Luxembourg Compromise on Majority Voting

An innovative clause of the Spinelli Project that was not included in subsequent Treaties is Article 23(3) that provided for the maintenance of the "Luxembourg Compromise" to prevent majority voting for a transitional period of ten years (should a vital national interest be recognized as such by the European Commission). Nevertheless, traces of this provision, which confirms Spinelli's political realism, can be found in the so-called bridging clauses, which provide for the passage from unanimity to qualified majority after a certain number of years (see Article 67 of the Treaty on European Union). Even the temporary revival of the so-called Ioannina mechanism in the Lisbon Treaty is inspired by the philosophy of the Spinelli solution.

The Designation of European Commissioners by the President

This provision of the Spinelli Project (Article 25) was not taken up again in successive Treaties. Nevertheless, it is an idea that had already been formulated by Valery Giscard d'Estaing during the European Convention on the Future of Europe and proposed again by French president Nicolas Sarkozy in his speech in September 2006 in order to appoint a Commission independent of nationality and not subject to the regular rotation of the Member States. In this case, too, this is a proposal that was ahead of its time.

The Primacy of European law

Article 42 of the Spinelli Project articulated the primacy of European law over that of the Member States. This provision, which results from the jurisprudential decisions of the European Court of Justice, was taken up again in Article 6 of the Constitutional Treaty of 2004.

The Elements of the Spinelli Project Still Unincorporated in the EU Treaty System

Other innovative provisions of the Spinelli Project were not acknowledged in subsequent Treaties or in the Constitutional Treaty of 2004. For example:

The System of Financial Equalization

Article 73 of the Spinelli Project made provision for a system of financial equalization to alleviate excessive economic imbalances between the regions of the Union. Inspired by the German federal system as a way of attenuating differences between the *Länder*, this provision was not acknowledged in successive amendments of the Treaties.

The Entry into Force of the Treaties

Article 82 of the Spinelli Project provided for the possibility that the Treaty should enter into force even in the absence of ratification by all the Member States. A majority of States representing two-thirds of the combined population could decide on its entry into force and on relations with Member States that had not ratified it. This clause set out to modify the unanimity ruling imposed today by Article 48 of the Treaties. Even though not acknowledged in subsequent Treaties, it triggered other solutions put forward to sidestep the need for unanimous agreement (see, for example, the solution proposed in the "Penelope" Project drafted by a group of European officials headed by François Lamoureux at the request of President Prodi).

Revision of the Treaties

Article 84 provided for a procedure to revise the Treaties through an agreement between the European Parliament and the Council in accordance with the procedure applicable to organic laws. This provision sought to remove from Member States the power to revise the Treaty and to abolish the need for unanimity. This procedure has recently been put forward again by MEP Andrew Duff for the new Constitutional Treaty.

The System of Revenues

Article 71 of the Spinelli Project foresaw the possibility of creating new revenues for the Union without needing to amend the Treaty (an organic law being sufficient). Moreover, the Commission would be authorized by law to issue loans. This proposal, highly innovative at the time, remains so even today.

Conclusion

A rough estimate shows that about two-thirds of the innovative provisions of the Spinelli Treaty have been adopted in subsequent Treaties. As far as the remaining third are concerned, about half were incorporated into the Constitutional Treaty and ultimately included in the Lisbon Treaty that is now in force since the end of 2009. This rereading of the Treaty of 1984 not only proves the vital importance of the Spinelli Project, it also underlines its farsightedness. Altiero Spinelli began the process of constitutionalizing the European treaties and proposed innovative solutions that have, for the most part, been adopted or recognized as valid solutions for the new Constitutional Treaty. Even though initially Spinelli lost the immediate battle of the Single European Act of 1986, we can say that today he has won the war to give the European Union a Treaty that is essentially, if not formally, constitutional and one which contains most of the solutions imagined by him and voted for by the European Parliament in February 1984.

CHAPTER TWO

Taking "Constitutionalism" and "Legitimacy" Seriously

Stefano Bartolini

"The name of the song is called 'LEGITIMACY.'"

"Oh, that's the name of the song, is it?" Alice said, trying to feel interested.

"No, you don't understand," the knight said, looking a little vexed. "That is what the name is called. The name really is, 'DEMOCRACY.'"

"Then I ought to have said 'That's what the song is called?" Alice corrected herself.

"No, you oughtn't: that is quite another thing! The song is called CONSTITUTION; but that's only what it's called, you know!"

"Well, what is the song, then?" said Alice, who was by this time completely bewildered.

"I was coming to that," the knight said. "The song really is TREATY: and the tune's my own invention."[1]

The recent debate surrounding the Treaty Establishing a Constitution for Europe and the subsequent Lisbon Treaty has been framed around the question "a constitution Yes or No" and the language of constitutional and legitimacy theory. This chapter argues that we should not discuss whether the EU has a "formal" constitution or not, but rather whether the EU treaties embody the principles of "constitutionalism" as developed by the European Enlightenment tradition. These principles include limited government, a bill of rights and judicial review, checks and balances and separation of powers, and, last but certainly not least, "the normative construction of political responsibility." Judged by these standards, the EU treaties, independently from whether we call them a constitution or not, are definitely defective on "constitutionalist" grounds because they very poorly substantiate these fundamental principles. This chapter does not argue that constitutionalism *should* be introduced into the EU architecture, although an argument to this effect can be made. It argues rather that words such as "constitution" and "legitimacy" should not be abused for a context in which "constitutionalist" principles are distinctively weak or absent altogether. Such verbiage is detrimental to the extent that it confuses and bewilders European citizens and it raises expectations or fears that cannot be either fulfilled or dissipated.

Introduction

In the middle of the 1980s two events spelled out clearly the alternative ways ahead for European integration. On the one hand, in early 1984, the "Treaty project establishing the European Union" fostered by Altiero Spinelli and his associates proposed a constitutional foundation for a federalist union; it failed. On the other hand, another project started immediately after to complete the internal market with a large set of directives and a common currency, and was successfully completed via the 1986 Single European Act (SEA) and the 1992 Maastricht Treaty.

Spinelli did not use the word constitution and the treaty project associated with his name was not called constitutional. Yet, it was a constitutional foundation for the following fundamental innovations: (1) it instituted a clear separation between two legislative chambers voting by majority (the Parliament and the Council, the second by weighted majority) and an executive (the Commission); (2) it clearly established the political responsibility of the Commission in front of the Parliament; (3) it introduced a difference between an organic law (mainly reserved for the organization and functioning of the Union's institutions) and normal legislation (mainly referring to the policies); (4) it endowed the Union with a fiscal power via an organic law; (5) it introduced the principle of treaty ratification by a simple majority of countries representing two-thirds of the Union's population.[2]

The choice to complete the market via the SEA and create a common currency under a substantially unchanged (or a piecemeal improvement of the) institutional framework was an opposite but equally clear and coherent choice. Many would also argue that it was a more realistic choice. Indeed, had Spinelli's project been approved, the completion of the market would have been more difficult and controversial. Yet the completion of the market immediately made the political question resurface again: can a European market made by intergovernmental agreements be later constitutionalized and politically legitimated?

In fact, following Maastricht, the words "constitution," "constitutionalism," "constitutionalization" spread in the discourse of the European political and administrative elites, were highly cultivated in intellectual and academic disputes, and eventually filtered into public and media debates. The issue of and the very terms "legitimacy" and "legitimation" had a similar fate, evincing the growing concern with the constitutional foundation and legitimacy bases of the Union.

The decade of intense treaty reform after Maastricht eventually led to the 2003 Convention on the Future of Europe, to its grandiloquent Constitutional Treaty, to its ratification by the EU member-state governments, and to its eventual disavowal by the people of two countries. The politically expurgated version of the Constitutional Treaty, the Lisbon Treaty, will come into force in early 2010 although its ratification still required a second referendum in Ireland, following voters' initial rejection of the treaty in 2008.

Therefore, in slightly more than twenty years, two attempts to establish a constitutional foundation for the Union have been defeated: the Spinelli Project, approved by the European Parliament and not labeled "constitutional," was defeated by the member states' governments; the Constitutional Treaty, approved by the governments and explicitly presented as a constitutional pact, was defeated by the people.

However, the similarity is misleading. While Spinelli's project was an attempt at constitutional foundation and federalist legitimacy, the Constitutional Treaty, notwithstanding its labeling, presented few constitutional features if any. It did not institute a clear separation between two legislative chambers voting by majority and an executive; it did not establish firmly the political responsibility of the Commission in front of the Parliament; it did not introduce a difference between constitutional law (the organization and functioning of the EU's institutions) and normal legislation (ordinary policymaking instruments); it did not endow the EU with fiscal power; and it did not overhaul the principle of treaty ratification.

In this chapter, I discuss the reasons and implications of the slippage from the prudence of Spinelli in the mid 1980s of constitutionalism without an explicit constitutional text, to the imprudence of today's supporters of a "constitutional" terminology in the absence of constitutionalism. To elucidate the basis of this slippage into verbiage with limited substance is essential not only to understand fully the trap in which the integration process is now snared, but also to avoid repeating the mistake of not taking constitutionalism and legitimacy seriously, something that perhaps the European publics have instinctively felt.

The "Strange Case" of European "Constitutionalism"

The terms "constitutionalization" and "constitution" intrude into the European integration literature and jargon through the work of international law and international relations scholars. Pointing to the *principles* of supremacy and direct effect of EC law and the constitutional authority of the Court of Justice[3] and referring to the evolutionary *process* from an arrangement binding only states into a regime of judicially enforceable rights and obligations on all legal persons and entities,[4] these scholars underlined that the treaties and EU law were becoming part of the legal order of each member state. Even in the absence of an EU-wide administrative apparatus and of direct instruments of implementation, the enforcement of European law, could be "defended" and "upheld" at the national level by those individuals who perceive a stake in it. National courts progressively made community law operative within the legal order of member states.

The second stream of scholarship and thinking that contributed to the spreading of the term "constitution/constitutionalism" in reference to the EU was that of neoliberal economics. In the normative language of this school the market-making freedoms, competition law, and more generally the activity of economic boundary removing are regarded as the essence of an "economic constitution." Economic competition and individual contractual rights are primary goals to limit "rent-seeking" activities in an enlarged cross-national market. Policies aiming to secure specific results are considered as prone to becoming the target of rent-seeking activities, even if they are not initiated this way.[5] Following these premises, the "constitution" of the EU is identified with the originally limited economic rights associated with the Common Market, and market-correcting policies are considered in a negative light. The hierarchization of rights and the constitutionalization of the market predefines the goals that individuals and groups are allowed to pursue, and precludes the formulation of public policies that encroach on such goals and rights. At the same time, this position "solves" the question of the constitutional foundation by grounding the legitimacy of the EU on fixed ontological economic liberties and rights.

More recently, a further contribution to the spread of the use of the term "constitution" has come from constitutional lawyers of the positivist school. Their argument is that the EU already has a "constitution," whether we call it this or not. The "constitution" of the EU is represented by those treaty norms that concern the general objectives, the allocation of competences, and the performance of legislative, executive, and judicial functions.[6] Political practicalities and expediencies aside—using the word "constitution" puts national political elites in a difficult position vis-à-vis domestic public opinion and may lead to ratification problems—the EU treaties *are* the EU constitution. This view contests the idea that the term "constitution" should be reserved for states, as indeed some well-known international organizations call their founding legal documents a constitution. In this formal sense, a "constitution" is fundamentally that "set of norms in a legal system which is more stable in terms of alteration of procedure than the (subordinate) rest of the legal order."[7] Therefore, the EU has a constitution, which is indeed made up by those articles of the treaties that pertain to the general objectives, the competences, and the legislative, executive, and judicial functions of the Union. On these premises, whether treaties are publicly called "constitutions" or "constitutional" is only a matter of political opportunity and expediency.[8]

The fourth main contribution to the spread of the "constitutional" terminology was the eagerness of large sectors of the EU technopolitical elite to adopt it. The constitutionalization jargon offered the impression of a major turning point in the history of the EU and of a newly funded source of legitimacy for further expansion of supranational policies. The declining public support for EU institutions and the many setbacks in referendums and European elections since the Maastricht Treaty have made these circles acutely aware that the integration process can no longer progress without more explicit popular support. The temptation to resort to the appeal of the terms such as constitution and constitutionalization was irresistible. Via an increasing resort to it in interviews by functionaries and politicians, it eventually made its way through the Convention on the Future of Europe and its adventurous decision to define its output as capable of "establishing a Constitution." This was a macroscopic attempt to rejuvenate support for the EU without facing the impossible task of agreeing on its true constitutional foundation.

In conclusion, sources for the widening use of the terms "constitution/constitutionalism" were disparate and the motivations diverse: (1) the intellectual surprise and fascination for the unexpected intrusion of international public law into national legal systems; (2) the attempt by neoliberal thinkers to seize the EU opportunity to establish a higher-order economic constitution able to weaken from outside the nation-state's "rent-seeking" activities; (3) the reduction of "constitution" to the higher echelon of an hierarchically ordered set of norms typical of positivistic legal theory; (4) the attempt by a wide section of the European political and administrative elite to renew the source of legitimacy of EU activities without unbalancing the delicate intergovernmental equilibriums too much.

To these components, one should probably add a certain amount of fearful complicity amongst European intellectual and academic milieus, generally with a positive orientation toward European integration and a strong awareness of the difficulties of the project. The fear of providing anti-EU ammunition often made them prisoners of the traditional wartime dictum: "silence, the enemy is listening to you." Not much intellectual debate surrounded this spreading use of the constitutional jargon and few critical voices rose against it or anticipated the risks implicit in it.

Yet there would have been ample room for that criticism. From the point of view of constitutional history and of the history of political thought the "constitutional" labeling as applied to the EU and its treaties, including the last one explicitly labeled "constitutional," would have been regarded as too audacious, if not misleading.

In the history of constitutionalism on both sides of the Atlantic[9] this term has meant limited government; a set of principles[10] to limit or otherwise circumscribe the previously unbounded and unconstrained powers of absolute rulers. The people who agitated throughout Europe asking for a constitution between 1830 and 1848 aimed at obtaining some guarantees against the abuse and arbitrariness of power, and a government limited by some general principle. The goal was to legalize power by offering a special protection to specific liberties of the governed. There is no doubt that this is the fundamental meaning of the term in the tradition which rests on the *Federalist* (1787–1788), the *French Declaration of Rights* (1789), and the classic systematization of constitutional thinking by Benjamin Constant in his *Cours de Politique Constitutionnelle* of 1818–1820.

The goal of limiting arbitrary power was achieved (more or less efficiently) with varying combinations of basic techniques: responsible government (linked directly, to the people, or indirectly to legislative assemblies), a bill of rights, judicial (and constitutional) review, and control, separation of powers.

In the Philadelphia Convention's constitution making, the principle of the separation of powers took on both a vertical and a horizontal dimension. The fundamental structuring principles were the center-periphery relations—and the vertical power attribution between the federal center and the federated states—and the horizontal distribution of powers, among the federal governmental institutions (Congress, President, and Supreme Court).[11] In the European experience the pre-existence of a centralized government and of a strong executive meant that the division of power principle was mainly institutionalized in the balances among central institutions (mainly government and parliament), while the territorial vertical division of powers was historically less important (with the exception of Switzerland).[12]

The essential goal of constitutionalism was *the normative construction of political responsibility*—who is responsible for decisions—and following this, *the identification of the target of positive and negative orientations*—who should be praised or blamed for those decisions—and, closing the circle, *the positive and negative sanctions associated with perceived misbehavior*.

In the European Union Treaties—prior to the approval of the introduction of the Charter of Fundamental Rights and Freedoms as an external but legally binding document in the Lisbon Treaty—there has been no bill of rights tradition. There is a strong center-periphery institutionalization of powers. This focuses on the prerogatives of the Council, but it is accompanied by a rather weak and technically formulated subsidiarity clause, that makes reference to "efficiency" in problem solving, more than to the autonomy and prerogatives of each level of government. Notwithstanding the increasing resort to the co-decision procedure and the growing role of the European Parliament as a legislator, there remains a blurred separation of powers among the central institutions (Council, Parliament, and Commission). Moreover, the respective role of these central institutions (including this time also the Court of Justice) changes dramatically from one policy area to the other. The procedures for the different decision-making areas and arenas are so complex and intricate as to make impossible a clear perception of political responsibilities. Any attempt to explain these rules to the broader publics beyond the restricted set of experts who interpret them is bound to fail.[13]

The Commission cannot be defined as the "executive" of the Union. It has a few features of an executive: (1) an administrative bureaucracy to prepare decisions and to monitor to some extent their implementation and enforcement; (2) a principle of political responsibility in front of the European Parliament, that can dismiss a Commission with a two-thirds censure vote; (3) it is appointed by the European Council (all national executives are appointed by a different body); (4) it does not decide but presents decisions to other bodies (no national executive decides; all refer their proposals to other bodies in order for them to decide); (5) it does not always have the legislative initiative (no national executive has such a monopoly). The fundamental differences between national executives and the Commission reside in (1) the lack of "constitutional competences" to propose the institutional architecture and policy competences of the Union, a power that no national executive is deprived of; (2) its monopoly of legislative initiative in various fields, a prerogative not enjoyed by national executives; (3) the Commission's exclusion from vast areas of Union decisions reserved for the Council(s).[14]

The Council, on the other hand, resembles a second state-based legislative chamber, in those areas where it is charged with the final approval of legislative initiatives of the Commission. Similarly, it has the typical legislature's powers to both initiate and conclude "constitutional" (treaty) revisions. Contrary to national legislative bodies, it has considerable limitation of its formal right to initiate legislation in several areas. The Council is sometimes seen as a branch of a dual EU executive. As such, it is even more atypical. No other different body appoints it. In several areas, it does not refer to any other body for final decision and approval. The co-decision procedure implying the search for agreement with the European Parliament resembles more the legislative *navette* of symmetric bicameral systems, than any known executive-legislative relationship. The Council is not politically responsible as a body in front of any other body (individual members can be, but the Council as such is not). Its composition is fixed and its members are ex-officio members. As an executive, the Council(s) also lacks the bureaucratic infrastructure to be able to process the high burden of administrative preparation of the decisions. Unquestionably, however, the Council(s) is both the executive and legislative in certain policy areas.

Considering the limitations to responsible government, the absence of a bill of rights tradition, the blurred separation of powers, the constitutionalization of the EU treaties is best represented by the foundation of the European legal system operated by the European Court of Justice's jurisprudence. However, this judicial review only applies to a subset, however important, of the EU activities. Only the core (first pillar) activities of the EU are defended in this way,[15] and despite the Lisbon Treaty's abolition of the pillar architecture other policy areas, notably foreign and security policy, will remain insulated from jurisprudence.

A further peculiarity makes the EU treaties very different from constitutions: the actual content of the protected core. National constitutions define basic rights and duties, the procedures for selecting those who are allowed to take decisions, and the formal procedure for taking decisions. As far as the substantive fields of decision making and the substantive goals of the decisions are concerned, constitutions are normally parsimonious. Many of their provisions are devoted to defining those areas in which the freedom of political decisions is constrained by higher principles, the protected core. Outside these constraints, constitutions say little or nothing about the actual content of what has to be done, where it is legitimate to do something. Every area not constitutionally protected is in principle subject to political decision making. In other words, national constitutions tend to be procedurally oriented and goal-independent.

The EU treaties define institutions and procedures to take decisions, but they are also largely devoted to a list of substantive goals in specific policy areas fundamentally aiming at the formation of a common market on a continental scale. There is no clear legal distinction between these two sets of norms. The "constitutionalized" international treaties include a large set of predefined substantive goals, whose implementation has its own logic and its own constitutional defense. The areas where the community has no competence are defined negatively, by omission.

"Constitutionalizing" the Treaties via judicial review has therefore meant to constitutionalize certain specific goals, shielding them from any political pressure or redefinition that does not embody a treaty change and does not muster the unanimity or the overwhelming majority of nation-states' executives. Therefore, we have a constitutional court for a nonconstitutional text that is atypical with respect to all known constitutions. Private and public actors have been constitutionally empowered, but only with respect to a predefined set of goals.

Paradoxically, the definition of the Communities as having the target of creating a common market implied a very broad (rather than a very narrow) perspective on the Community activities. Everything depends on what is defined as "common market" (e.g., public services, health, labor contracts, etc.). This definition is left to intergovernmental negotiations and there is little that can defend other institutions or actors from what the national governments decide by unanimity.

What has been said above is not meant to be a critique of the current institutional architecture of the EU. It is a critique of the undue application to it of the term "constitution" and, even worse, of the term "constitutionalism." We can agree to call the architecture of the Union as its "constitutional structure" only if we give to the term "constitution" a purely descriptive and formal meaning: this is the way the EU institutions work and relate one to the other. However, in mistaking or substituting the term "constitution" for the essence of "constitutionalism" we pay a preposterous price. There are plenty of historical and contemporary examples of states, which are undoubtedly states, which have constitutions, which are undoubtedly called constitutions, and which are totally unconstitutional in their text, spirit, and working.

That constitutionalism is something more than basic economic rights, a hierarchy of norms, or a description of the functioning and competences of whatever political institutions is further demonstrated by the fact that constitutionalism soon became a structure of political legitimation. Indeed, it became one of the two most powerful sources of political legitimation in Western political thought and institutional development (the other being, of course, electoral competition). Constitutionalism then became "constitutional legitimation," that is, a way to legitimize collectivized and binding decisions. Constitutionalism is inextricably linked to the principles of modern and rational political legitimacy.

The Multiplication and "Crumbling" of the Principles of Legitimacy

In its encounter with the EU, the concept of "legitimacy" has suffered a similar fate as that of "constitution/constitutionalization." Its meanings have been multiplied and stretched, and its principles have crumbled. Even in this case, therefore, a return to the original meaning may help to orientate ourselves in the maze. The concept of legitimacy refers to—and was invented for—the fundamental predicament of politics: when and why should people accept and abide by collectivized and binding decisions in the formulation of which they have not participated or, while participating, have seen their preference unsatisfied?

Following this, legitimacy is clearly unnecessary and immaterial whenever decisions are not collectivized; that is, when the actors concerned and affected are left with exit options, with the possibility to avoid the application and consequences of the decisions. Legitimacy is equally unnecessary and immaterial when decisions are based on the consent of the actors who have an effective veto power on disliked decisions: unanimity. In short, legitimacy problems emerge only in conditions of no exit or no unanimity.

Given that the operational definition of legitimacy as the likelihood of obedience remains elusive and shows its importance only in extreme situations and only *ex post*, most debates about legitimacy focus on the principles and the procedures through which it can rationally be argued that collectivized decisions must be accepted by those who have seen their values or preferences unsatisfied. Today, our capacity to rationally argue about the binding nature of the rules is still largely shaped by constitutionalist principles: if, the extent to which, and when these decisions have been reached following the principles of constitutionalism. In this sense constitutionalism is at the core of modern sources of legitimacy, that is, at the core of all rational arguments concerning the conditions of obedience to political decisions. Therefore, deliberatively or inadvertently confusing the term "constitution" with the term "constitutionalism" attributes to a descriptive, formalistic concept the precious value of a source of political legitimacy. Which is exactly what I argue should be avoided.

Given what has been said above, it is not surprising that, although constitutionalism is a crucial root of political legitimacy in Western thought, it does not play a role in the debate about the conditions in which EU decisions must be accepted and acquiesced to by dissenters and nonparticipants—the debate about the political legitimacy of the EU. In fact this debate has followed three main streams, none of which takes on board constitutionalism: (1) it has denied the need for sources of political legitimacy; (2) it has argued for "special" and *sui generis* legitimacy sources; (3) it has advocated a political legitimacy resulting from partisan and adversarial behavior within the main EU institutions. Indeed, this absence of constitutionalism among the sources of EU political legitimacy is the best sign of its weakness in the EU institutional framework.

The EU Does Not Require "Political Legitimacy"

The first camp argues that the intergovernmental nature and action of the EU does not require any additional legitimacy beyond that indirectly offered by the voluntary consent of the member states and the ratification processes of their national parliament. To the extent that the EU is based on a voluntary agreement to participate, leaves open a constant exit option to all members, allows partial exits, contracts out, variable geometry and the like, resorts to unanimity voting and/or to mechanisms of disproportionate weights on many issues, then legitimacy is immaterial within the EU and there is hardly any need to discuss it. Yet, the spread of QMV in the Council(s), the growing legislative powers of the European Parliament in several fields, and the ECJ-guided "constitutionalization" process transform collective unanimity decisions into collectivized decisions that some member states and groups of citizens have to accept. If decisions are not always unanimous and exit options are progressively reduced, legitimacy problems reemerge.[16]

A different version of the "no need for political legitimacy" position stresses the intrinsic nature of the decisions, rather than the procedure for their articulation. It is argued that in the sphere of "efficiency issues" the delegation of decision-making powers to independent institutions (i.e., not electorally legitimized) is justified and does not require further legitimation. For such issues, "efficiency" is more important than political legitimacy, therefore competence, expertise, procedural rationality, transparency, accountability by results, and so forth, are sufficient to legitimize the EU and to justify the delegation of necessary powers.[17] This reasoning boils down to two points: some issues, for their technicality or complexity, are surrounded by some general consensus on the goals to be achieved and incompetence about the means to do so. This consensus on the goal is arrived at without asking anybody about it. There will be therefore a range of issues and decisions for which debates among experts are insulated from any political decision-making process and debate.

This idea effectively denies the fundamental predicament of the political—how can people arrive at and accept collectivized decisions starting from different values and preferences—by arguing that people "do not have" or "should not have" different preferences and values in certain fields and issues. By assuming that values and preferences do not need to be ascertained and by predefining a number of goals to which efficiency maximization logic is applied, the political predicament disappears. The problem with this elegant solution is that competence legitimizes decisions in matters where individual values and interests are easily defined in generalizable terms (interest in health, safety, survival, etc.) and as such can be "predefined."[18] In many other areas people disagree on what "efficiency" is, which are the efficiency issues, and on whether experts' decisions are more appropriate than political negotiations to achieve efficiency. Provided this disagreement exists, we need to invoke a higher conflict resolution principle to solve the problem. The competence/efficiency formula is a removal of the problem, more than a solution to it.

The EU Has "Different" but "Adequate" Legitimacy Sources

A second position suggests that EU activities are not deprived of legitimacy but are sustained by "a different kind" of legitimacy, and should be judged by different standards than those of national political legitimacy [19] Within the general but weak "infrastructure of political accountability" offered by national and European elections,[20] other mechanisms, alone or in conjunction, can be utilized to sustain the legitimacy of the EU outputs.

The first of such mechanisms is represented by "corporatist and intergovernmental agreements" for the determination and control of rule application in certain domains. The specific feature is the wide participation of affected and concerned parties and interests that control some crucial resource. With the broad participation of all (or almost all) affected interests, the need for legitimacy is actually reduced, according to the elementary rule that the more inclusive the input for decisions the less necessary is any legitimation of it. With a slight switch of emphasis, it is also argued that decisions taken by this method are legitimate because they are more effective in reaching their goals. In other words, the specific kind of input (the involvement in the decision of those interests that control key resources for its implementation/enforcement) does guarantee a more effective output. In this way, "effective" (*nota bene*: "effective," not "efficient") implementation is regarded as a source of legitimacy. However, for effectiveness to be a source of legitimacy it requires that the goals of these arrangements are accepted and appreciated by the public who does not participate in the decisions. However, if the goals are accepted and appreciated the problem of legitimacy is resolved already, *ex ante*.

Another typical mechanism of legitimacy is the resort to independent expertise, as already discussed previously. In this case, expertise is not presented as a way to escape the legitimacy problem for efficiency-defined issues, but it is seen as an additional element among many others that contribute to the legitimacy of the output. Competence, as opposed to political equality and affected interests participation, is a well-established principle of authority and source of legitimacy whenever everybody prefers to follow the advice of recognized authorities rather than to accept different decision rules. It is based on the recognition of strong asymmetries of knowledge and experience and on the acceptance of the requirements that stratify access to the credentials for such knowledge and experience.

An additional mechanism invoked as producing EU legitimacy is that of the "public policy pluralist networks" involving concerned interests with open access (not restricted to major representative organizations) and the largely informal process of exchange of information and critical appraisal of different options which contribute to the elaboration of public policies. The legitimizing aspect of policy networks is deemed to be the associational pluralism *à l'américaine* and the process of deliberation and public discussion that make it possible to define consensually "generalizable interests." These public policy networks describe more informal interaction models that precede, accompany or follow the formal decisions rather than describe the formal institutions of decision making. The argument is that network interactions eventually improve the quality of public policy choices.

Summing up this argument, in a concise way that does not do justice to its complexity, one can conclude that new forms of "governance" based on negotiated agreement among affected interests, mediated by experts' advice, open to a wide process of exchange of information and critical appraisal of different options may lead to more effective implementation of policies and this, in turn, may constitute a source of legitimacy for the wider polity. To capture this phenomenon, Fritz Scharpf has coined the imaginative term of "output legitimacy."[21]

The European Commission has invested considerable symbolic and material resources in the new governance mechanisms and there is no doubt that it has added to the mere intergovernmental legitimacy of early times. Nevertheless, there remains a certain ambiguity between criteria like the effectiveness of implementation, the quality of policy making, the efficiency of outcomes, and legitimacy *tout court*. Moreover, this line of argument somehow equates the consent and agreement of the affected and involved with the acquiescence of the uninvolved. Finally, it seems unlikely that these mechanisms can be effective in conflict resolution in those areas that appear more controversial: the constitutive EU issues of membership, decision rules, and competences.

In general, one should not overemphasize the EU's specificity in resorting to these mechanisms of governance. National democracies do not rest on the principle of electoral legitimacy alone,[22] but on a plurality of concomitant and parallel mechanisms that complement one another in different functional areas. Most of the decisions at the national level, as much as in the EU, are shaped if not formally taken via these governance tools, rather than via political-parliamentary decision making.

The overarching difference between the EU and the nation-state does not lie in the presence/absence of corporatist agreements, competence bodies and policy networks. It lies in the centralized convertibility of the resources each of them exchanges. Votes (and the principle of political equality) can be weighed against the control of implementation and enforcement resources of the relevant organized interest, and the latter against the former. Expertise and procedural competence and the role of genuine deliberation *fora* also play a role in specific functional areas predefined by other decisional principles and spill over their effect even outside them. The holders of different kinds of resources the politicians and the voters, the bureaucrats and the interest representatives, the experts and the judges exchange continuously their respective assets in a situation in which ultimately none of them can subtract themselves from collectivized decisions fundamentally resting on the principle of political equality. These "political" decisions are therefore not the principal or main form of decision making, but rather the guarantee of the convertibility of a plurality of resources and legitimacy principles. In the context of the EU, missing the element of political legitimation, the other principles are not complementary, but self-sustaining.

Legitimation by Increasing Politicization and Partisanship

On the basis of the argument of the previous sections, therefore, a growing number of experts and also European politicians have argued for a third solution that they perceive by now as necessary and/or unavoidable: legitimacy problems can only be solved by politicizing the EU, via the introduction of a greater dose of political electoral responsibility for those who take decisions. The injection of stronger elements of partisanship and majoritarianism in the EU consensual processes is expected to (1) foster the development of partisan alignments in its main institutions; (2) make political mandates clearer; (3) help overcoming coordination problems among the key institutions (Council, Commission, Parliament); and (4) link citizens' interests and preferences to the EU's internal debates. Great expectations are placed in the idea of a more open contestation of the office of the Commission President, and of the key positions in the Commission/Parliament, allowing alternative candidates to declare their programs before the EP elections, issuing manifestos for their term of office, and forcing parties to declare their support for one or the other candidate. It is expected that these results can be achieved by piecemeal changes that, while increasing issue politicization, do not change the basic institutional architecture of the Union, for which there is obviously no unanimous consent.[23] For this politicization to have the expected beneficial effects and to avoid unexpected negative ones, a number of conditions have to be met, which are quite demanding.

First of all, we should make sure that politicization will spare the "constitutional" or "constitutive" issues of the EU concerning membership (the geographical boundaries of the Union), competences (what should be done at the EU level as opposed to other levels of government), and decision-making rules (how collective decisions should be taken) and will focus only or mainly on issues similar to the national issues (levels and types of market regulation, welfare, citizenship rights, immigration policy, law and order issues, etc.). So far, national parties and electorates divide more often on European constitutive issues than on isomorphic issues. In the thirty-six referendums held between 1972 and 2003 in the member and candidate countries, the profound splits among party leaders and between party leaders and their electorates have affected both right and left wing parties and have all resulted from the politicization of the constitutive issues of membership and new treaty ratification.

We also need to trust Euro-parties (parliamentary groups and federations) to be capable of offering a coherent and significant left-right alignment and competition and handle the delicate gatekeeper task that the politicization thesis attributes to them. Notwithstanding the thesis that they are strengthening in cohesion and partisan discipline, it is far from clear that they can effectively perform the work of representational channels. It is at least doubtful that their delicate internal equilibriums would sustain and survive a strong politicization of the EU agenda. These types of Euro-parties, rather than being the key agencies of politicization, could be its first victims.

Third, if the more open and contentious exposition of different platforms and agendas generates the sense of a political mandate for the electoral winner(s), this should then be reconciled with the narrow policy boundaries of the treaties and with the predefined goals of the EU (see section *supra* on "constitutionalism"). Such mandates risk being frustrated by the autonomy of the European Central Bank, by the case law of the ECJ, by the blocking vetoes in the Council, by treaty-specified duties and competences. These treaty obstacles may generate such intense political frustrations that they would immediately spill over to the institutional constraints that make it impossible to implement the mandate politically defined. The argument that the political mandate so defined will be accepted by those on the losing side in the expectation that in the future they may be on the winning side is therefore rather visionary and abstract, and it could raise expectations that cannot be satisfied.

Even the idea that political mandates can coordinate policy positions across EU institutions—the Council, Commission, and Parliament—and help to overcome institutional gridlocks among them is doubtful. The coordination of policy positions thanks to partisan alignments has to overcome the disturbing element of commissioners appointed by governments no longer in charge and of Councils changing political orientation during the life of a European Commission and Parliament. The different timing of formation and composition of these bodies will generate permanent and unstable "divided government," changing directions and intensity in an unpredictable and relatively random way. As things stand, clear-cut partisan alignments may not solve problems of cross-institution coordination, but may add problems of political and partisan coordination to the already existing problems of institutional coordination.

Finally, we are also unsure as to whether the emerging pattern of left-right politicization will link more solidly citizens' interests and preferences to EU politics. For sure, any politicization of integration/independence issues would probably increase the gap between parties and voters, and split and tear apart Euro-parties. In any case, politicization may generate excessive hopes and expectations, to be frustrated later and widen the gap between normative expectations and reality.

Taking Constitutionalism and Legitimacy Seriously

The distrust and mutual horizontal control among member states and the competition between authorities in a composite polity represent a source of effective control over the EU activities. New forms of governance focusing on affected interests' participation, corporatist agreements, expertise and competence evaluation, epistemic communities, and policy networks may be enough to legitimate the output of the EU in a number of areas. If we deem that the standards of national democratic legitimacy are too high and inappropriate for the EU, we may hope that increasing partisanship in appointments at the top and in the functioning of the parliament/commission may attenuate public perception of the distance and remoteness of EU institutions, without raising excessive expectations. However, taken individually, classic intergovernmentalism, modern technocracy, old and new forms of governance, and the drive toward partisan politicization are insufficient to rationally argue the legitimacy of the growing political production of the EU. Taken together and combined these principles reinforce one another and help to support such political production.

The accumulation of all these practices, however, is neither constitutionalism nor legitimacy and does not solve satisfactorily the political predicament embedded in the definition of the goals and major activities and decisions within the EU. The terms are stretched, misused, and abused, but the underlying problem is hardly solved and perhaps it is even exacerbated. The resulting system is overly complex, arcane to its citizens, and unable to contribute to the normative construction of political responsibility, which I have argued is the keystone of constitutionalism.

From an historical perspective, it is easy to understand how this came about. In the first period, the segmented definition of EU competences required only that the various programs be developed by the cooperation of functional elites that, on the basis of specific criteria of economic rationality, enjoyed a large immunity from public opinion, interests and national positions. The politics of integration was based on the assumption that the technical policies based on economic rationality were beneficial for all participants. This politics did not require nor resort to value representation and discourses of a noneconomic type. A consensus toward the economic regulations of the exchange relationships was sufficient to the construction of this segmented community guided by criteria of economic rationality.[24]

The expansion from the early core, however, was pursued without clear-cut constitutional guidelines—such as those enshrined in Spinelli's 1980s proposal—but with the same segmental logic. This eventually led to the pluralization of the treaty regimes and to the intertwining of levels of decision making in different sectors. This has progressively made more difficult the understanding of this dynamic system, which is not only multilevel, but also multi-loci.

In fact, in certain policy areas the competences, activities, and legislation of the EU have gone so far that any constitutional foundation cannot be achieved without accepting the idea that such *acquis* be called into question, challenged, and eventually modified. In other areas, on the contrary, the *acquis* is so meager and subject to member states' approval and their mutual veto and mistrust that it can hardly be submitted to a constitutionally legitimate principle of decision. Having created a market as a set of predefined rights and goals against considerable national resistance and cheating, we need to recognize honestly and publicly the difficulty to "constitutionalize" and "legitimize" this *ex post*. The EU system is largely based on the internal disciplining and mutual mistrust and control among member states. Any attempt at effective constitutional legitimation is likely to upset and unbalance this delicate mechanism of inter-elite control.

In every process of constitutional legitimation the normative construction of political responsibility and a system of sanctions is necessary. The difficulty of identifying the rationality criteria in a complex system, the crumbling image of those who hold hierarchically ordered competences with territorial sovereignty, the vagueness of the relationships of interdependence breaking up the specific value references, render very difficult, if not impossible, the constitution of any element of negative or positive political identification, without which "politicization" cannot occur. Calling this system "constitutional" can only increase the dissatisfaction and the fear of citizens.

Euro-skeptical positions are often criticized for their lack of focus, for their lack of specific grievances, for their lack of specific redress requests, for their being more a "mood" than a program or a specific issue disagreement, and so forth. However, the nature of this euro-skepticism should come as no surprise. How could it be different given the nature and the complexity of the system that has been created? How could it be different when the institutional architecture and the policy process make it difficult to distinguish to whom to attribute responsibility and to whom to direct expectations?

Perhaps part of the European publics and elites want a constitutional foundation and part do not, but I feel that both parts instinctively dislike the current tendency to cheat and not take constitutionalism seriously. The result is that continuing the debates and the reform attempts under this discourse and terminological ambiguity is likely to generate opposition and resentment on both sides. Those who fear or dislike a constitutional foundation feel that the increasing resort to these terms points to clear intentions and an unfolding reality. Those who aspire to a constitutional foundation perceive the ambiguity of intentions and the inadequacy of reality behind the abuse of words.

This chapter does not propose practical solutions to go ahead and get out of the current vexing situation. The chapter only warns against the dangerous tendency to hide the clear terms of the current critical juncture by stretching, adapting, abusing, and misusing concepts such as constitution, legitimacy, democracy, political mandates, and so forth. The misleading conceptualization that recently flourished in parallel to the attempt to reform the treaties is appealing because it has proven successful at the national level. European citizens and voters have done the only thing they could do: they have read these discourses with their national understanding of the terminology, while realizing that the corresponding institutional underpinning was, or should have been, absent in the EU. Therefore, this warning is not issued for the sake of theoretical coherence, conceptual clarity or linguistic purity, but because the persisting ambiguities and uncertainties about the European constitutional foundation *are a policy mistake*.

The beginning of a fresh debate about the future of the EU's institutional architecture requires reflection on and understanding of the mistakes of the past before taking new action, especially after an extended period of activism and advancement without adequate reflection and understanding. This is a formidable intellectual task and one in which scholarly circles have a crucial role of rigorous critical evaluation to play, a goal toward which this chapter makes a modest contribution.

Notes

1. Adapted from Lewis Carroll, *Through the Looking Glass* (London: Puffin Books, 1984 [1872]), 51.
2. Treaty Project Establishing the European Union, *Official Journal of the European Communities*, 19 March 1984.
3. The Court of Justice has pointed to the EC Treaty as the "constitutional charter of the European Community" in one of its cases (Case 294/83 *Les Verts versus European Parliament*).
4. Joseph Jupille and James A. Caporaso, "Institutionalism and the European Union: Beyond Comparative Politics and International Relations," *Annual Review of Political Science* 2 (1999): 429–44, 440.
5. See Manfred E. Streit and Werner Mussler, "The Economic Constitution of the European Community: From 'Rome' to 'Maastricht,'' *European Law Journal* 1, no. 1 (March 1995): 5–30 as an example of this line of reasoning applied to the EU treaties.
6. See, for instance, Koen Lenaerts and Piet van Nuffel, *Constitutional Law of the European Union* (London: Thomson/Sweet & Maxwell, 2005).
7. See Stefan Griller, "Fundamental Approach of the Lisbon Treaty. Is this a Constitution?," discussion paper presented at the conference "The Lisbon Treaty and the Future of the European Constitutionalism," Florence, European University Institute, 11–12 April 2008.

8. For a similar line defining constitution making as the activity of regulating matters that are more fundamental than others, attributing to a text the special status of primary law source, defending and shielding such a text from transformation by the requirement of stringent amendment procedures, see Jon Elster, "Ways of Constitution-Making," in Axel Hadenius, ed., *Democracy's Victory and Crisis* (Cambridge: Cambridge University Press, 1999), 123–42. These characteristics, however important, do not seem to me essential in defining the goals of constitutionalization.

9. For a review of this history see Giovanni Sartori, "Constitutionalism: A Preliminary Discussion," *American Political Science Review* 56, no. 4 (Dec. 1962): 853–64.

10. Generally "written" but not always so, as the English case shows. However, a great deal of what could be called the British constitution has a written form (Magna Charta, Confirmation Acts, Habeas Corpus Act, Bill of Rights, Mutiny Act, Toleration Act, Act of Settlement, and others) although it is not formalized in a single written document.

11. The "right to be protected" (the Bill of Rights) was added later with the first ten amendments approved by the two chambers of Congress in 1789 and finally approved by the states in 1791. The amendments have become twenty-seven since then. See the literature in Sergio Fabbrini, "Transatlantic Constitutionalism: Comparing the U.S. and the EU," paper presented at the Transatlantic Studies Conference, University of Dundee, Scotland, July 8–11, 2002.

12. This explains why in the United States competition was largely articulated in institutional terms, between federal and state institutions and between central federal institutions, while in Europe competition was more based on central political conflicts between majority and opposition, political parties and in general centralized political actors.

13. For an excellent discussion of the continuing, if not growing, "complication" of the EU legal instruments and decision-making procedure see Bruno de Witte, "Sources of Law and Law-Making in the Lisbon Treaty" (discussion paper presented at the conference "The Lisbon Treaty and the Future of the European Constitutionalism," Florence, European University Institute, 11–12, April 2008).

14. No similarity exists between the practice of *domaine réservé* in dual executives and the circumscription of the Commission's role in the second and third pillars. The former more appropriately applies to those Commission acts that do not require the approval of the Council and the Parliament. For a discussion, see Jean Blondel, "Formation, Life and Responsibility of the European Executive," paper presented at the University of Catania, workshop on "Democrazie ed Elezioni nell'Unione Europea," May 1999.

15. That is why, perhaps, to describe the EU as a confederal institutional arrangement and a federal legal arrangement is going too far. See Joseph H. Weiler, "Federalism without Constitutionalism: Europe's Sonderweg," in *The Federal Vision. Legitimacy and Levels of Government in the United States and the European Union*, ed. Kalypso Nicolaïdis and Robert Howse (Oxford: Oxford University Press, 2001): 54–70, 58.

16. Andrew Moravcsik, "In Defense of the 'Democratic Deficit': Reassessing the Legitimacy of the European Union," *Journal of Common Market Studies* 40, no. 4 (Dec. 2002): 603–34; Andrew Moravcsik, "Is There a 'Democratic Deficit' in World Politics? A Framework for Analysis," *Government and Opposition* 39, no. 2 (Spring 2004): 336–63.

17. Giandomenico Majone, "Europe's 'Democratic Deficit': The Question of Standards," *European Law Journal* 4, no. 1 (March 1998): 5–28; *Regulating Europe* (London: Routledge, 1996); "The Regulatory State and Its Legitimacy Problems," *West European Politics* 22, no. 1 (1999): 1–24.

18. Even in the most obvious cases of generalizable public interests, however, the credentials to competence and the mechanisms to access those credentials may be challenged and refused.

19. Adrienne Héritier, "Elements of Democratic Legitimation in Europe: An Alternative Perspective," *Journal of European Public Policy* 6, no. 2 (June 1999): 269–82.

20. I refer here to Fritz Scharpf, *Governing in Europe: Effective and Democratic?* (Oxford: Oxford University Press, 1999), chapter 1.

21. For an extended discussion of the utility of the concept of "output legitimacy" see Stefano Bartolini, *Restructuring Europe. Centre Formation, System Building and Political Structuring between the Nation State and the EU* (Oxford: Oxford University Press, 2005), 165–75.

22. See Stein Rokkan, "I voti contano, le risorse decidono," *Rivista Italiana di Scienza Politica*, 5 (1975): 167–76.

23. Andreas Follesdal and Simon Hix, "Why there is a Democratic Deficit in the EU: A Response to Majone and Moravcsik," *European Governance Papers* (EUROGOV 2005) No. C-05-02, www.connex-network.org/eurogov/pdf/egp-connex-C-05-02.pdf (accessed 15 October 2009); Simon Hix, "Why the EU Needs (Left-Right) Politics: Policy Reform and Accountability Are Impossible Without It," paper for *Notre Europe*, Paris 2006 (www.notre-europe.asso.fr).

24. M. Rainer Lepsius, "Integrazione economico-politica e pluralità culturale," *Il Mulino Europa* 2 (February 1997): 3–18, 8.

PART TWO

THE COMPARATIVE DIMENSION

CHAPTER THREE

Revisiting Altiero Spinelli

Why to Look at the European Union through the American Experience

Sergio Fabbrini

Altiero Spinelli was not a scholar. He was a knowledgeable person, but mainly interested in political action.[1] However, he understood what the mainstream of European studies continues to misunderstand, namely that the experience of European integration has deep similarities with the one which has taken place in the United States.[2] In 1957, Spinelli wrote "notwithstanding the diversity of particular problems to face, and their relative simplicity in the American case, the birth of the United States is of fundamental importance for the Europeans because in that experience it is possible to see, as *in a laboratory* (*come in un'esperienza in vitro*, in Italian, italics mine), the basic factors of a problem that democratic Europe has to face today" (my translation).[3] Yet, this view notwithstanding, the European Union[4] has been interpreted, at least by two generations of scholars, although belonging to different approaches (neo-functionalism, intergovernmentalism, constructivism), as a case of "institutional exceptionalism," or "*ad hoc* polity," or "post-modern polity." The outcome has been a detailed knowledge of the branches and trees of the EU, but a scarce comprehension of the EU as a wood, that is of its *nature*. European studies are running the risks, well known to the critics of U.S. political science,[5] of becoming redundant and parochial.

Although Altiero Spinelli was insightful in looking at (the birth of) the EU through the United States' experience, nevertheless he did not have, in 1957, sufficient historical material for pursuing the comparison to a full extent. If it is true, as Spinelli argued in his essay, that the main difference between the United States and the EU derives from the fact that the former started from a *constitutional* choice and the latter from a *functional* strategy, nevertheless it is also true, as Spinelli did not envision in the same essay, that the constitutional origin of the United States has not resolved once for all its problems of *finalité* and, at the same time, the functional foundation of the EU has not impeded its subsequent constitutionalization.[6] Indeed, both polities have had to face contestation about the nature of their constitutionalization, although the existence (in the United States) and the nonexistence (in the EU) of a formal constitution have differently affected the systemic implications of that contestation. The United States and the EU have witnessed a contested process of constitutionalization because both are asymmetrical unions of states (and their citizens). This asymmetry is an expression not only of the different size of the constitutive units (*material asymmetry*), but also of their different history (*cultural asymmetry*).

Asymmetrical unions of states and their citizens have to organize according to a different democratic model than the ones adopted by nation-states. I argue that the United States and the EU represent different species of the same genus, that of the *compound democracy*. It is not federalism that is the defining feature of the United States nor is quasi-federalism the defining feature of the EU, but it is the multiple separation of powers' system that defines both of them (and distinguishes both of them from other federal nation-states).[7] In institutional terms, the United States and the EU have developed similar institutional features, separating decision-making power vertically and horizontally, a multiple separation of powers made operative by the mechanism of checks and balances. Certainly, the EU is a union of states which *de facto* has adopted a *compound democracy* model, whereas the United States has adopted this model *deliberately*. Nevertheless, in both cases, because of their compound nature, it has been impossible to find a definitive solution to the dilemma of their constitutional identity. Constitutional disputes have been the norm in the United States since its founding and have become the norm in the EU with the starting of the constitutional project in the 2000s. However, the different constitutional setting of the United States and the EU has contributed to generate, out of those disputes, different systemic outcomes in the two polities: centripetal in the United States (of course, after the bloody Civil War of 1861–1865) and centrifugal in the EU. In the United States, a centripetal outcome has meant the gradual amendment of the constitutional pact. In the EU, a centrifugal outcome has meant the formation of periodical situations of stalemate in the process of defining the nature of the constitutional pact.

Here, I will try to pursue the comparison between the EU and the United States, *revisiting Spinelli's comparative view*. For doing that, I need (section 2) to show that the EU may be compared to the United States because it is a democratic and constitutionalized polity. On this basis, I will then analyze the American (section 3) and European (section 4) experience of institutional compoundness and contested constitutionalization. Finally, I will derive (what I consider as) the crucial analytical indication from this comparative exercise, *thus redefining Spinelli's comparative view* (section 5).

Compound Democracy and Constitution

Is the EU Democratic?

Interpretations of the EU abound, although many of them are not helpful for understanding why its treaties dealing with constitutional issues (such as the organization of institutional powers and the definition of fundamental rights) were so deeply contested.[8] The EU has faced contestation because it is much more than a regulatory system,[9] a governance system[10] or a federalizing system.[11] The constitutional difficulties of the EU are not simply characteristic of a political system,[12] but of a political system with democratic features.

A polity is democratic when it meets basic criteria of representation and accountability. Regarding the first criterion, those who take decisions in the EU were elected either by citizens in national elections (members of the Council of Ministers) or European elections (members of the European Parliament), or nominated by politicians elected in national and European elections (members of the European Commission). Moreover, EU decision makers are compelled to act within a complex system of separation and balancing of powers, which was gradually defined by the various treaties, and they are subject to the control of national constitutional courts and the European Court of Justice (ECJ). Finally, they have to face periodical evaluation by the electorate, thus satisfying the criteria of both inter-institutional and electoral accountability. Certainly defining the EU as a democratic polity does not mean shielding it from criticism. However, such criticism needs to be placed in the context of the democratic model adopted by the EU. A democratic model concerns the way in which systemic divisions are institutionally and politically translated into authoritative decisions applicable to all members of the polity. The EU, however, has come to be organized along a democratic model that is very different from the ones adopted by its member states.

The democratic models of the EU member states fall into two polar categories: the majoritarian/competitive model and the consensual/consociational model, with some EU member states oscillating between the two.[13] These two models reflect the different nature of the existing cleavages in European societies. The majoritarian/competitive model characterizes countries such as the United Kingdom where material (economic, social) divisions are more salient than other divisions, and where the main political actors share a homogeneous political culture. The consensual/consociational model, in contrast, characterizes countries such as Belgium where cultural (linguistic, ethnic, religious) divisions are the most salient, and where the political actors do not share a common political culture. In both models, however, parliament is the only institution expressing popular sovereignty. Or better, both democratic models are characterized by a government, *as a single institution*, that reflects the political majority of the parliament, regardless of whether it is formed through bipolar electoral competition or through post-electoral negotiations among the main actors of a multiparty system.

The EU's model of democracy is quite different. I define this model as compound democracy.[14] A compound democracy is a democracy *for a union of states*, whereas the democratic models of the EU member states are characteristic of *nation-states*. The compound nature of the EU is due, not only to the aggregation of distinct states *and their* individual citizens, but above all, to the *asymmetric* nature of these units. In the EU, the main divisions are between territorial units, that is, member states, rather than between social classes or cultural communities.[15] In asymmetric unions of states, ultimate authoritative decisions are reached through the cooperation of multiple separated institutions. Contrary to the fusion of power systems of all EU member states, separation of power systems do not dispose of *a government as a single institution*. In the EU sovereignty is fragmented, pooled and shared by several separated institutions. The Council of Ministers, the Commission, and the Parliament (and more and more the European Council) represent different electoral constituencies, if not concurrent majorities, and operate on the basis of different temporal mandates. Nevertheless they are constrained to share decision-making power.[16] Given the separation among the institutions that structures the decision-making process and the number of actors involved, it is highly implausible to establish "who has to be considered responsible for what" in the EU. This is why, since the 1970s, the issue of the "democratic deficit" of the EU has been raised. However, if one takes into consideration the systemic constraints of a union of asymmetrical states, then this criticism would seem misplaced. Even in its federal form, a union of asymmetrical states cannot be organized along the vertical lines of a parliamentary model. Parliamentary federalism is possible only where the territorial units are relatively alike in terms of demographic size and economic capability, for example, in post–Second World War Germany whose *Länder* were designed by the Allied authorities in order to prevent the more populous ones from gaining control over the legislature on a permanent basis.[17]

Is this model unique? Indeed, if the EU is different from its member states, the same cannot be said regarding other unions of states, such as the United States and Switzerland. Also the United States and Switzerland, like the EU, do not have a *government as a single institution*. Also in the United States and Switzerland, as in the EU, the decisions are taken through the participation of different and separate institutions. If we stick with Spinelli's comparative aim, one may therefore argue that, in institutional terms, the EU displays more similarities with the United States than with its member states. Both the EU and the United States are polities with a highly complex structure of multiple separations of powers in order to keep on board states of asymmetrical size and culture.[18] Having defined the democratic model of the EU, it is now necessary to identify its constitutional basis.

Is the EU a "Constitutionalized Regime"?

The concept of constitution is not as unequivocal as it might seem. From the perspective of Comparative Politics, we can distinguish, at least, between a formal and material constitution.[19] A *formal* constitution is a single written document that it is regarded (by governed and governors alike) as the supreme text of the legal order, it regulates matters that are more fundamental than others, and it may be changed only through stringent amendment procedures.[20] Although all formal constitutions establish the set of fundamental rights, institutional arrangements, and functional procedures that must regulate the workings of a given political community (which constitutes itself through this founding document), one might argue (as Elazar does[21]) that important differences are detectable among them. In fact, some formal constitutions (such as the American one) are first a *frame of government* and then a protector of rights (indeed, the Bill of Rights is a set of ten amendments added to the formal document two years after its approval), while other formal constitutions (such as the ones approved in post–Second World War Europe) have the features of a *state code*, the expression of a declared democratic ideology (indeed, the French or Italian constitutions start with a definition of fundamental rights and end with a specification of powers and procedures to preserve them).

On the contrary, a *material* constitution consists of the social practices, derived from political conventions, historical traditions, specific judiciary regulations or ad hoc fundamental laws (considered of an equivalent status to a constitution) recognized as the basic norms of a given society. It is the case of democratic countries like the United Kingdom, Germany, or Israel: in the first case the material constitution is constituted by an historical accumulation of ordinary laws and judicial sentences considered of fundamental importance for the polity, in the other two cases by an ad-hoc fundamental law (called *Grundgesetz* in post–Second World War Germany).[22] Evidently the EU does not have a formal constitution, but it is indisputable that it does have a material constitution consisting of the juridical expression of high-order principles (such as the supremacy of Community law or the direct effect of Community law on individual citizens) established by the ECJ on the basis of the treaties and recognized as such by the member states and their citizens.

Thus, the ECJ has interpreted the founding treaties as quasi-constitutional documents, and these rulings have gradually been integrated into the constitutional orders of the member states.[23] Contrary to other international treaties, the EU treaties have therefore given rise to a legal order which not only binds the governments that signed them (as is typical of international treaties) but which is also of direct influence on the citizens of its member states.[24] At the same time, through the various Intergovernmental Conferences (IGCs) organized since the mid-1980s, the heads of state and government of the European Council have introduced several institutional reforms in order to fine-tune the functioning of the decision-making structure, if not to adapt the latter to the changes activated by the judicial decisions of the ECJ.[25] Accordingly, one might argue that this material constitution has sustained a process of *constitutionalization*, where the latter has to be interpreted as "an exclusively descriptive concept (indicating) the recollection of constitutional norms, rules and decisions"[26] recognized as the basis of the polity. However, stressing the empirical quality of the process of constitutionalization, intended as the creation of a functional integrated legal order in a given political territory,[27] cannot imply considering it equivalent to a formal constitution, as is recognized by several authors.[28] A material constitution can properly function where the symbolic role of a formal constitution is not necessary, because citizens' identification with the polity comes from historical meta-constitutional sources (as was the case with United Kingdom, Israel and Germany). Compound democracies cannot rely on meta-constitutional sources.[29]

The ECJ has used the opportunities afforded by the treaties to construct a new legal order for a supranational market, transforming those treaties into sources of law superior to those of the EU member states.[30] The heads of state and governments, frequently in response to problems emerging from the policy-making process, have used IGCs and European Council meetings for clarifying the roles and competences of Brussels and domestic institutions.[31] This constitutionalization has gradually transformed the European nation-states (with a few exceptions among the established democracies, such as Norway and Switzerland)[32] into *member states* of the EU. The traditional European nation-states have had to redefine their sovereignty by sharing it with other nation-states within the context of the EU institutional structure. If sovereignty coincides, at least empirically, with the power of taking ultimate decisions, the nation-states of Europe, becoming EU member states, have come to share this ultimate decision-making power (on several policies affecting their own societies) with institutional actors external to each of them (the other member states' representatives in the two Councils and the members of the Brussels Commission and the Parliament). Thus, empirically, each EU member state has remained sovereign in some policy fields (very few indeed) but not in others (quite a few indeed).

If the EU is a constitutionalized compound democracy, nevertheless it differs in a crucial way from the other constitutional compound democracies, such as Switzerland and the United States. Following Spinelli, the crucial difference between the EU and the United States resides in the fact the latter is based on a founding document and its amendments (the *constitutional text*), whereas the former is based on successive interstate treaties. Constitutionalization based on interstate treaties, originally intended to create an economic union (a common market), is significantly different from constitutionalization based on a constitution formally intended to create a political union.[33] However, this difference has had different implications than those envisioned by Spinelli. Rather than ending the disputes, the United States constitutional text has furnished a normative language for framing the divisions on the nature of the constitutional order (at least after the Civil War of 1861–1865) that have continued, whereas in the EU the interstate treaties' basis of the polity has not been able to frame the normative discourse on its nature. Moreover, while the constitutional text of the United States has allowed for the use of super-majority criterion for emending it, on the contrary the interstate treaties of the EU have imposed the unanimity criterion for changing them, thus making the dispute on the future of the EU's constitutional order highly uncertain. Because the United States provides the first historical experience with compound democracy, it is necessary to start the comparison there in order to better identify the problems besetting the constitutionalization of a compound democracy.[34]

Compound Democracy and Constitutionalization in the United States

The American Experience with Compoundness

Whereas the EU is a compound democracy by necessity, the United States is a compound democracy by design. Indeed, James Madison called it a compound republic. Although it is legitimately assumed that the American constitution celebrates a covenant among citizens ("in America . . . it is the People who are the source of rights,"[35] it is nevertheless important to stress that it was a covenant among citizens *organized into distinct states*.[36] As Forsyth has explained, "neither the preamble, nor Madison's successful endeavor to provide the constitution with a deeper foundation than that of a normal treaty between governments, prevented it from being considered from the start as a species of contract or compact. Ratification was unequivocally a matter for each state individually; none could be bound without their assent."[37] The U.S. Constitution is the first *peace pact* among republican (or democratic, we would say today) states of different demographic size, material capabilities, and cultural values (e.g., slavery). As Hendrickson has written, "it seems fair to denominate the federal Constitution as a peace pact, the most unusual specimen of this kind yet known to history."[38] It is a pact designed to anticipate possible conflicts among independent states located on the same territory. In fact, had a conflict broken out, the independence of all states would have been jeopardized, because of the interests of the great European powers to play off one state or group of states against the other.[39] Thus, the United States represents the first attempt to avoid a repetition of the experience already familiar from Europe at the end of the eighteenth century, namely the inability of balance of powers systems to prevent war.[40]

In Philadelphia, constitution makers decided to neutralize such a threat by constructing a polity that combines inter-states and supra-states features. In the United States, "the Constitution created a Republic of different republics and a nation of many nations (and) the resulting system was sui generis in establishing a continental order that partook of the character of both a state and a state system."[41] This polity necessarily had to be open to different and changing policy outcomes. A union of asymmetric states can prosper only by hampering the formation of permanent majorities.[42] Such majorities should be able to emerge only when there is an overwhelming consensus in the country, something that historically has occurred only in the wake of major domestic or international crises or traumas. Finally, the Philadelphia constitution was approved by a large majority of the states, but not by all, through legislative decisions or ad hoc constitutional conventions. Indeed, the U.S. Constitution cannot be subjected to the examination of states' popular referendums.

Because the United States aggregates previously independent states, it is not surprising that the constitution only defines the few competences of the federal centre, leaving all the rest to the federated states.[43] In order to assure all the would-be members of such a union, the delegates at Philadelphia devised an institutional system of vertical and horizontal separation of powers able to prevent the formation of factional majorities, with the Supreme Court as the guardian of that structure. All of the separated institutions, both at the centre (President, House of Representatives, and Senate) and in the states (governors and bicameral legislatures),[44] were endowed with independent legitimacy: direct legitimacy in the case of the House of Representatives, indirect in the case of the President and the Senate until 1913. In addition, each institution has its distinct operational time span. Accordingly, no institution depends on the others in order to function and none of them requires the confidence of the others in order to perform its tasks. As Neustadt has written, in Philadelphia "a government of separated institutions sharing powers" was created.[45] Moreover, the power of *judicial review* implies that every decision taken by the legislature and countersigned by the President can be annulled by any court that considers it to be unconstitutional.[46] This has never been the case in the European nation-states.[47]

The American constitution introduced a hierarchy of norms without, however, introducing a corresponding hierarchy of institutions or organized powers. In particular, it did not solve the question of the relation between the federal state and the federated states, as became evident with the outbreak of the Civil War in 1861. To be sure, for the first century of the new republic, Congress played a much more relevant role than the President and the federated states were much more influential than the federal state (*congressional government*). However, since the 1930s and especially since the end of the Second World War, the President has become pre-eminent vis-à-vis the legislature as has the federal centre vis-à-vis the states (*presidential government*).[48] However, the increasing role of the President has not diminished the power of Congress.[49] Indeed, with the full institutionalization of the presidency, the United States has become a fully separated governmental system,[50] and the increasing role of Washington, D.C., has not prevented the states from playing a more influential role in policy making since the 1970s.[51] The power pendulum has continued to swing back and forth.[52]

Defining a hierarchy of norms in Philadelphia was not a simple undertaking because of diverging state interests and views on the union. The absence of a clear correspondence between norms and institutions does much to explain the failure of the first U.S. Constitution of 1781 (known as the Articles of Confederation), and the dramatic crisis of the second one (with the Civil War of 1861–1865). However broad the consensus on a supreme legal text may have been at Philadelphia in 1787, it was much more limited with respect to fundamental issues relating to the relations between the "new" centre and the "old" states and the separate institutions within them. Contrary to the interpretation that the United States was a "naturally" homogeneous country (as John Jay ideologically argued in the *Federalist no. 2*, when he stated "that Providence has been pleased to give this one connected country to one united people—a people descended from the same ancestors, speaking the same language, professing the same religion, attached to the same principles of government, very similar in their manners and customs"),[53] the United States was and has continued to be a highly divided polity for all of its history, with the main divisions concerning the nature of the union.[54] Periodic waves of immigrants, with their distinct "manners and customs," have regularly fed the divided nature of the country.

Since the Philadelphia Convention, therefore, the United States has gone through cyclical crises of constitutionalization that generally pitted groups of states against one another on specific issues. This was so in the 1830s with regard to the role and independence of the federal bank; in the 1860s regarding the sovereignty of the states in imposing slavery; in the 1930s regarding the role of the federal Congress and the President in regulating the economy; in the 1960s regarding the recognition of civil rights in the Southern states; and finally this was the case in the 2000s regarding the powers of the President and Congress to restrict the rights of citizens for reasons of national security. In all these conflicts cleavages have emerged between small-medium and larger size states; between states with solid democratic cultures and states with racial preferences; between states promoting a continental market and states with protectionist outlooks; and, *especially*, between states favoring a stronger federal role and states claiming their own prerogatives in a confederal perspective.

Constitutional cleavages between states not only triggered a dramatic Civil War, but have continued to structure the main political divisions of the country.[55] More frequently the contrasts were between sections or regional groups of states, rather than between single states. In the United States, these sections or groups of states are distinguishable for their specific economic-productive basis[56] or peculiar cultural identities. Indeed, utilizing the criteria of political culture, Elazar has managed to identify at least eight sections of the country: New England, Middle Atlantic, Near West, Northwest, Far

West, Southwest, Upper South, and Lower South.[57] The political parties have contributed to taming these territorially based constitutional divisions because they have been inclusive confederations of different state and local interests rather than tools for the exclusive ideological mobilization of the electorate as in Europe.[58]

Moreover, territorial conflicts have frequently overlapped with cleavages concerning the democratic nature of the political system. For a large part of the nineteenth century some defenders of the states' powers as well as critics of the federal centre's power had argued that, for obvious geographical reasons, only the states could ensure citizen participation in decisions. At the end of the nineteenth and the beginning of the twentieth century, criticism of the federal centre's democratic deficit assumed very different features. Having been forced to acknowledge the process of nationalization that had traversed American politics (e.g., decisions increasingly came to be taken in Washington, D.C.),[59] the critics of the democratic deficit set out to democratize the federal institutions. The Progressives and the Populists therefore advocated reform of both national and local systems.[60] In sum, in the United States, constitutional divisions have been a permanent feature of the political struggle.

The American Experience with Constitutionalization

Although different views and interests of the states have characterized the political development of the United States, nevertheless the constitution has furnished a procedure for solving them, albeit temporarily, without jeopardizing the compound nature of the polity (again, after the Civil War of 1861–1865). Certainly, the translation of a political majority into a constitutional one has been effectively constrained by the principle of the *double super majority* required for passing amendments. Article V stipulates that "whenever two thirds of both Houses shall . . . propose amendments to this Constitution [the proposal] will be valid to all intents and purposes as part of this Constitution, when ratified by the legislatures of the three-fourths of the several States, or by conventions in three-fourths thereof, as one or the other mode of ratification may be proposed by the Congress." However, the principle of a double majority does not equate with unanimity. In fact, it has not proven insurmountable, as shown by the twenty-six amendments approved so far at the federal level.

Indeed, the ink on the constitution was not yet dry when the Americans began to discuss the need to amend it.[61] The ten amendments known as the *Bill of Rights*, introduced, as we know, two years after the Philadelphia Convention, have ushered in a permanent discussion on the constitution.

If twenty-six amendments have been approved so far, thousands more were proposed. Yet, no amendment has called into question the structure of multiple separation of powers characteristic of the U.S. compound polity, nor has any political leader ever called into question the legitimacy of the principle of a double super-majority for changing the constitution. In fact, some of the amendments have changed specific properties of single institutions (like Amendment XVII of 1913 on the direct election of federal senators, or Amendment XXII of 1951 which states that "No person shall be elected to the office of President more than twice"); others have introduced a new interpretation of the fundamental rights (implicit or explicit) to be protected (like Amendment XIII of 1865 which abolished slavery, Amendment XIV of 1868 which imposed the respect of basic rights to the states, or Amendment XV of 1870 which recognizes that "The right of citizens of the United States to vote shall not be denied or abridged by the United States or any State on account of race, color, or previous condition of servitude").

When reforms did aim to alter the compound nature of the republic, such as the proposal to substitute the Electoral College (an institution which overrepresents the small states because of the unrepresentativeness of the Senate)[62] with the direct election of the President, the stringent amendment rules have enabled the opposing coalition (of small states' representatives and electors) to thwart these proposals. Notwithstanding events in Florida during the presidential elections of 2000, the abolition of the Electoral College is still considered impracticable today. Moreover, when the process for amending the constitution became politically rigid, owing to either the formation of conservative majorities able to control both chambers of Congress, or to the formation of veto minorities in one of the two federal chambers, or in the state legislatures, major constitutional changes were introduced via other channels, such as rulings by the Supreme Court, the latter now being considered an integral part of the constitution.[63]

Although constitutional disputes have been a constant feature of the United States, these conflicts have been waged through a shared constitutional discourse, in particular (of course) after the Civil War. Because of the trauma generated by that war,[64] those contenders have used the language of the constitution in order to legitimate their claim, thus mobilizing different interpretations of the constitution in regard to issues of the day. The constitution's language has delimited and defined what should be considered the legitimate political discourse. In sum, although Americans have come to recognize the constitution as the basis of their staying together, this has not been based on a common interpretation of the constitution but on the effort to justify the divergent interests and views with reference to the same constitutional text. Ackerman has written that "because Americans differ so radically . . . our constitutional narrative constitutes us a people."[65] The amendment procedure, though stringent, has finally furnished the "safety valve" allowing the constitution to be adapted to a changing environment,[66] if considered necessary by a super majority of federal and states' representatives (and, behind them, by a large majority of citizens).

Compound Democracy and Constitutionalization in the EU

The European Experience with Compoundness

The EU is a different species of compound democracy than the United States in terms of its "systemic foundations" (see table 3.1). Nonetheless, the logic of functioning and the institutional structure of the EU and the United States seem to be quite similar.

The EU started (with the Rome Treaty of 1957) as a project for building an integrated continental market. After the 1954 rejection of the European Defense Community project by the French Parliament, the main European political leaders of the time decided to promote the integration of the continent through economic means rather than political principles.[67] However, it was clear to the founding fathers of the (then) European Economic Community established by the 1957 Rome Treaty that Europe had to find a way to permanently close a long era of internecine civil wars.[68] Thus, the EU may also be considered as the outcome of a *pact* for promoting peace among traditionally warring states, a pact based on economic cooperation through a common market regulated by a complex institutional framework. Moreover, although the purpose of the treaties, especially of the 1957 Rome Treaty, was to create the conditions for a civil pact among traditional enemies, the latter had already established a military pact, tutored by the United States, through NATO (which was established in 1949 and then strengthened in 1955 with the integration of West Germany).[69]

Table 3.1. The U.S. and the EU: Systemic Foundations

	United States	*European Union*
Aim	to avoid possible wars	to close an era of wars
Justification	to create a political union	to create an economic community
Logic	fragmented sovereignty	pooled sovereignty
Structure	formally derived	pragmatically defined
Rationale	clear (*e pluribus unum*)	ambiguous (economic or political union)

After all, the balance of power logic of the traditional Westphalian system of states had proved to be the source of permanent interstate insecurity, thus triggering periodic attempts by individual states (the strongest ones at the time) to impose an imperial order on the continent. The European nation-states had to recognize that their best chance of avoiding war was to build a *novus ordo seclorum*, although they decided to start from economic cooperation in order to mature the conditions for a more advanced integration. What we now call the EU is an attempt to steal out from the Westphalian solution to interstates rivalry *without however giving a political justification* to that attempt.[70] Whereas the founding of the United States was based on a constitutional pact which celebrates the political reasons of the union,[71] the foundation of the EU lacked any political justification.

With the EU, nevertheless, for the first time in history, the European nation-states have tried to build an institutional order which combines intergovernmental as well as supranational features through negotiation over economic issues of common concern. In fact, as the historical experience had amply shown, the new order could not be guaranteed solely by an intergovernmental agreement, but it needed to be protected by supranational Community institutions. Without authorities institutionally separated from the states that had created them (such as the Commission, the Parliament and the ECJ), there could be no guarantee that the signatories to the intergovernmental agreement would abide by their own rules. In the EU, Community features are necessary for regulating interstate rivalries. In this sense, the EU has been an attempt to domesticate the external relations of the European nation-states, creating an international regime with domestic features.

If the foundations of the new order resided in transnational cooperation on a growing number of economic matters,[72] this cooperation has led nevertheless to the progressive institutionalization of the close network of Community institutions envisaged by the original treaties—the Council of Ministers, the Commission and the Parliament, the Court—but also institutions not originally envisaged, such as the European Council. The institutionalization of the structure of multiple separations of powers between the Brussels' institutions and between them and the institutions of the member states has strengthened the compound nature of the EU. Since the 1986 Single European Act (SEA), the 1992 Maastricht Treaty (which introduced a three pillar structure) and the 1997 Amsterdam Treaty, the EU has progressively become a system in which several institutions separately but jointly contribute to numerous public policy decisions. Before the 2009 Lisbon Treaty, that system of separated institutions concerned primarily the first pillar, while the other two pillars maintained a more intergovernmental nature.

Acknowledging the process of cross-pillarization which led these two pillars to be affected by the logic of the former,[73] the 2009 Lisbon Treaty has recomposed the three pillars in a unified legal framework, although it has made possible the adoption of different decision-making regimes in different policy fields (in particular in foreign and security policies the decision-making regime is mainly intergovernmental). In general, the 2009 Lisbon Treaty has defined more precisely the nature of the system of separated institutions (and it has recognized the Charter of Fundamental Rights as equivalent to a new treaty). Thus, the originally pre-eminent institution in the system, that is, the Council of Ministers, has been forced to acknowledge the considerable influence acquired by the Commission. In addition, it has been obliged to recognize the co-determination and co-decisional power acquired by the Parliament since its direct election in 1979, and especially since the SEA and the two fundamental treaties of the 1990s. The 2009 Lisbon Treaty has further strengthened that power. Those treaties have thus contributed to a deeper institutionalization of the separated decision-making structure of the EU. In sum, like the United States, the EU has come to function *without a government acting as a single institution*. In Brussels decisions are taken and values are authoritatively allocated, but this is the outcome of a process of negotiation and deliberation involving a plurality of actors and taking place within the loose confines of a system of separated institutions.

As a result of the progressive deepening of European integration, the EU is no longer the economic organization preferred by the intergovernmentalists, although it has not become the political union desired by the federalists. With the end of the Cold War and the prospect of the political reunification of the continent, given the ambiguous connotation of the EU, the dispute on the *finalité* of European integration has inevitably acquired a constitutional character. The necessity to define the constitutional identity of the EU emerged during (and after) the Intergovernmental Conference (IGC) held in Nice in December 2000 and whose treaty was signed in 2001 (European Council 2000). Recognition of a Charter of Fundamental Rights (though not its inclusion) in the 2001 Treaty of Nice has further stoked the debate on the constitutional nature of the EU. Given the unsatisfactory outcome of that treaty, the European Council held in Laeken (Belgium) on 15 December 2001 adopted a Declaration on the Future of the European Union that committed the latter to defining its constitutional basis (European Council 2001). Indeed, the Laeken Council convened a Convention in Brussels bringing together the representatives of both the member states' governments and parliaments and Community institutions with the task of preparing a draft treaty establishing a constitution for Europe for the 2004 IGC.

The Brussels Convention lasted from February 2002 to June 2003, concluding its activities with a unanimous agreement on the proposed Constitutional Treaty or CT.[74] On 18 June 2004 the heads of state and government of the member states reached a compromise on a slightly revised form of this draft. Because that treaty is the closest approximation to a formal constitution ever agreed by member states' governments, it has been rightly said that the outcome of the Brussels Convention has transformed the EU from a *constitutional project*[75] into a *constitutional process*,[76] the so-called Laeken process. This process has been highly contested. In fact, the CT was rejected in the French and Dutch referenda of May 29 and June 1, 2005, respectively, thus causing the EU to pause for reflection. The pause was concluded by the agreement reached in the European Council meeting held in Berlin in June 2007, which laid the ground for the signing of a new treaty in the following European Council held in Lisbon on 13 December 2007 (the Lisbon Treaty). The Lisbon Treaty has transformed a large part of the CT into a set of amendments to the two existing treaties and has recognized the Charter of Fundamental Rights as a *de facto* third treaty, discarding however all the symbolic features of the CT (such as the flag, the anthem, the preamble and, above all, the idea of a unified text).[77]

Subsequently, the Irish "No" to the Lisbon Treaty in the referendum of June 12, 2008, reopened a new crisis in the constitutional process, a crisis which seemed to deepen when the Czech and Polish presidents of the republic decided to withhold their signatures to the treaty already approved by the legislatures of those two countries. Moreover, the decision, taken in Germany, of submitting the Lisbon Treaty for an evaluation of its constitutionality to the German constitutional court (*Bundesverfassungsgericht*) made the process even more cumbersome. Nevertheless, these hurdles were bypassed. The German court, in a ruling of June 30, 2009, recognized the congruence of the Lisbon Treaty with the domestic constitutional order, though requiring a revision of the parliamentary law of approval of the treaty. That law should have had an explicit reference to a strengthened role of the German legislature in the EU decision-making process, a revision immediately introduced by the two chambers of the German parliament before the national elections of September 2009. In Ireland, a new referendum on the Lisbon Treaty was held on October 2, 2009, and a large majority of voters this time voted in favor of the treaty. Finally, the Polish president of Republic signed the treaty, followed by his Czech counterpart. Eventually, on December 1, 2009, the Lisbon Treaty became the new legal basis of the EU.

Constitutional Divisions in Europe

The Laeken process has been characterized by deep divisions or *cleavages* specifically concerning constitutional issues (such as which institutional form the EU should assume, which rights the EU should protect).[78] The various cleavages that had remained submerged during the long period of material constitutionalization of the EU have thus surfaced. Some of the conflicts that emerged during the Laeken process were of a temporary nature as the position of some member states on specific issues changed according to the government of the day. However, other divisions had a more permanent character, reflecting stable differences of views and interests among member states (and their citizens), due to their *material* asymmetry (different demographic and economic size) and *cultural* asymmetry (different history and political expectations).

The first of these structural cleavages concerns the division between large and medium-small member states. This conflict has surfaced regularly during the history of the EU: for example, in the 2000 Nice Treaty negotiations, when a medium-sized member state such as Spain was able to obtain very favorable conditions for the weighting of its votes within the Council of Ministers, thus benefiting future candidate states of equivalent size, such as Poland. The same has happened during the debate on the CT when Spain and Poland tried to maintain their favorable status (which overrepresented them) in the newly designed Council of Ministers. The compromise found in the Rome European Council of October 2004 (European Union 2004), namely that a decision of the Council of Ministers will be effective if supported by a majority of 55 percent of the member states representing at least 65 percent of the population, was subsequently challenged by Poland at the Berlin European Council of June 2007. In the Lisbon Treaty the Polish government obtained a deferral of the introduction of this rule to November 2014 with an additional transition period until March 2017, during which a member state can ask for a qualified majority on a specific issue if considered of national importance (Council of the European Union 2007). The same cleavage also emerged on the issue of the Commission's composition during and after the Brussels Convention.[79] The small and medium-sized member states obtained that each member state be allocated one commissioner whereas the large member states advocated setting the number of the commissioners to two-thirds of the member states. A first version of the Lisbon Treaty (article 17) established that the number of Commissioners be reduced, in the sense that only two out of three member states would have the right to representation on a rotating basis although postponing the introduction of this rule to 2014. However, after the refusal of the treaty in the first Irish referendum of June 12, 2008, the European Council decided to reinstate the clause of a number of commissioners equivalent to the number of member states, thus easing the approval of that treaty in the second Irish referendum of October 2, 2009.

The second structural cleavage has been the traditional one between the countries of western continental Europe and the countries of northern insular Europe. For years this cleavage has accompanied the process of European integration, in particular since 1973 when the United Kingdom, Denmark, and Ireland joined the EU. This cleavage reflects the different historical experiences of the western "islands" and the "continent" in the formation of the nation-state and its international extensions. The former consider the deepening of the integration process a threat to their national sovereignty, which is to be countered by pressing for further enlargement.[80] Although the process of Europeanization has curtailed the sovereignty of the member states on many public policies, this has not impeded some of them from defending their founding myths. In these countries, the defense of sovereignty springs from the distinct historical phenomenon of democratic nationalism: it is nationalism which has enabled them, and especially the United Kingdom, to preserve democracy.[81] Indeed, the United Kingdom, Ireland, Denmark, and Sweden have obtained several opt-outs from parts of the treaties in question. In exchange for signing the Lisbon Treaty, the UK government has obtained the right to opt out even from the Charter of Fundamental Rights and, together with the Irish government, it has also opted out from the change from unanimous decisions to qualified majority voting in the sector of Police and Judicial Cooperation in criminal matters.

The historical experience of the continental countries of Europe has been very different. Here, nationalism had erased democracy, owing to a set of cultural and geographical factors. The development of the democratic state encountered much more unfavorable conditions in the "land-bound" European countries than in the "sea-bound" ones.[82] In the former, nationalism was frequently anti-democratic, submitting to (or sustaining) the centralizing ambitions of dominant authoritarian groups. For the EU member states that inherited this historical experience and memory, integration represented the antidote to the virus of authoritarian nationalism, whereas those that have inherited the "island" experience view political integration as a threat to their democratic identity. It must be added, however, that large sections of the French elite regard integration mainly as an opportunity to promote a greater role for France,[83] rather than to check their nationalistic instincts. In this sense, the cleavage between these two Europes is also an effect of the competition between two traditional European powers, with the United

Kingdom traditionally in favor of a Europe firmly allied with the United States, and France favoring a Europe independent from, if not competing with, the United States.[84]

The third structural cleavage has opposed many citizens and significant sections of the political elites of the new member states of Eastern Europe to the old ones of Western/continental Europe. In particular, the nationalistic governments of some new member states, such as the Polish government of the period 2005–2007 and the Czech government that emerged from the 2007 elections, have been preoccupied with defending their regained national sovereignty after almost half a century of domination by the Soviet super-power. These governments seem to view the EU mainly as an open market in which they can remedy their economic backwardness without constraints on their political sovereignty. Their views, although frequently expressed in an extreme way, have tended to overlap with those of the northern "islands," thus giving increased strength to the originally minority position of the EU as economic organization. Certainly, these territorial cleavages are only indicative of the constitutional divisions existing within the EU. In fact, in the northern "islands" as well in the eastern member states there are those in favor of greater political integration, just as there are influential groups supporting only economic integration in western continental Europe. Moreover, EU constitutional issues have frequently intermingled with domestic issues or domestic political ambitions, as happened in the 2005 French referendum.[85] Indeed, referendums on EU treaties were an occasion for evaluating the incumbent domestic government, rather than for discussing the content of those treaties. Yet, these cleavages express relatively stable divisions concerning the constitutional future of the EU. It might be added, also, that these cleavages have not found a party-based representation coherent with the left/right division. When constitutional questions were at stake, the left/right division did not hold. The constitutional odyssey of the first decade of the twenty-first century shows the different implications of the constitutional divisions within the EU. Whereas the divisions deriving from the material asymmetries (demographic size, economic capability) have been somehow mediated, the divisions deriving from the cultural asymmetries (different perceptions of national identity and supra-nationalism) could not be mediated by a material constitution.

In conclusion, the constitutional conflicts produced regular constitutional stalemates in the EU because they were not framed by a constitutional discourse shared by the contenders and because they were not ordered by a non-unanimous (though stringent) procedure for solving them. Although the EU is no longer an international organization (as is shown by its material

Table 3.2. The U.S. and the EU: Constitutional Foundations

	United States	*European Union*
constitutional basis	constitutional text (founding document with amendments)	interstates treaties (interpretations by the ECJ and IGCs decisions)
constitutional change	double super-majority no states' popular referendums	unanimity states' popular referendums (some)
constitutional language	shared, integrative, inclusive	unshared, differentiated, idiosyncratic
constitutional divisions	internal to the constitutional pact	on the nature of the constitutional pact
constitutional outcomes	centripetal (after the Civil War)	stalemate (if not centrifugal)

constitutionalization), it has kept an amendment procedure which is specific to that organization. This unanimity procedure, which was viable when it was established in 1957 by the six founding nation-states of the EU, is an example of institutional path-dependency. Once introduced, a rule (or an institution) tends to remain in place, although it no longer serves the purpose for which it was originally intended.[86] Moreover, the constitutional requirement of some EU member states to hold a popular referendum before ratifying any new treaty has introduced a further hurdle to this procedural context. The suggestion made by the former European commissioner Mario Monti seems reasonable, namely that a referendum on EU treaties be acceptable only when a negative vote implies secession from the union.[87] It is not surprising that stalemate has been a regular outcome of the EU constitutional debate. Thus, although the EU and the United States have been both characterized by a contested process of constitutionalization, they have nevertheless registered different constitutional outcomes due to their different "constitutional foundations" (see table 3.2).

Conclusion

Through the comparison with the United States, Spinelli kept alive the idea that the EU was built not only for promoting a common market but for responding to the dramatic failure of the European nation-states. Indeed, Spinelli was one of the first European intellectuals to recognize that failure, writing about it (in 1941) on the Mediterranean island of Ventotene, to which he was confined by the Italian fascist regime. If the United States started out as a peace pact for preventing internecine collapse between newly founded republics (an attempt which failed with the Civil War of 1861–1865 and then was relaunched after that war), the EU started out as a peace pact for concluding a long and bloody sequence of European civil wars (guaranteed by the military pact organized within NATO). After the 1954 defeat of the project of a European Defense Community, the political rationale was downplayed by the founding European government of the then EEC. Spinelli was right in insisting that Europe would have needed something more than a neo-functional justification for developing successfully,[88] although it should be recognized that the neo-functional approach has allowed Europe to constitutionalize to an extent unforeseen by its federal critics. Spinelli's insistence on the necessity to arrive at a constitutional treaty has contributed to keeping open an alternative political view on European integration. With his Draft Treaty, approved by the European Parliament on February 14, 1984, he inspired the treaties of the 1990s and especially the 2004 CT. Without a formal constitutional pact, for Spinelli, the EU could not rise to the level of its responsibilities, namely to guarantee peace and to promote prosperity through the redefinition of the national sovereignties of European nation-states. The approval of a constitutional treaty was considered by Spinelli to be the necessary condition for overcoming the ever reemerging historical tensions between the European nation-states.

However, Spinelli's approach of looking at the EU through the United States experience needs revision. In fact, he misinterpreted the U.S. experience, overestimating the *power* of a formal constitution (or constitutional treaty) to end the constitutional disputes. In fact constitutional disputes have continued to shake the U.S. political experience, notwithstanding the existence of a formal constitution. The U.S. experience shows that a formal document is not sufficient *per se* for resolving the disputes on the nature of the polity, but it is necessary for making their outcome centripetal. The U.S. experience shows that those disputes are permanent in a union of asymmetrical states (and their citizens) organized along the institutional lines of a compound democracy. Compound democracies are inevitably contested polities. Their institutional structure keeps open the dispute because it lacks any centralizing mechanism. Those disputes are not a barrier against the consolidation of a compound democracy if they are kept within a shared constitutional language and if there is a procedure for solving them unconstrained by the unanimity criterion. A common constitutional language and super-majoritarian amendment procedures are the necessary conditions for neutralizing the centrifugal impetus of the constitutional divisions between states and between citizens. Certainly, the U.S. experience shows also that they are necessary but not sufficient conditions for promoting a centripetal outcome, as happened before the U.S. Civil War, when groups of member states and citizens spoke consistently different constitutional languages and did not consider legitimate the procedural criteria for solving them.

In the light of the U.S. experience after 1865, one might therefore argue that the opposition to an EU constitution or constitutional treaty should not in itself be a cause for concern. Rather a cause for concern should be the unwillingness of (some of the) contenders to agree with the idea that the EU should have a constitutional treaty on the basis of which to regulate the constitutional dispute. In fact, once the constitutional cleavage has become the predominant division of the polity, as has happened in the 2000s, then the EU can no longer rely on a neo-functional strategy for regulating the disputes on its *finalité*. Also European constitutional pluralism[89] does not suffice for guaranteeing a centripetal outcome from those disputes. It might be necessary for preserving the material constitution, but it is not sufficient for substituting a formal constitution. In order to deal with its internal divisions the EU, like the United States, needs both a shared normative frame and a viable procedural mechanism that only a formal document could provide (it does not matter what to call it, basic treaty, fundamental treaty, constitutional treaty, union pact).

Here is the difficulty. The divisions within the EU are too deep to arrive at such a document. The view of the EU as an *economic organization* and the view of the EU as a *political union* are too far apart to be reconciled in a common basic document. Certainly, one might argue that, through the activation of art. 1, paragraph 22, of the Lisbon Treaty (amendment of art. 10 of the 1992 Maastricht Treaty) which allows for reinforced cooperation between some member states in specific policy fields (such as foreign and security policies), the two views of the EU could find a reciprocal accommodation. However, this strategy does not necessarily guarantee to neutralize the centrifugal tendencies within the EU. Indeed, it might end up in periodical stalemates between the two Europes. In fact, if the supporters of the *economic* view are minded to veto any significant developments in the direction of a *political* union, at the same time the supporters of the latter are in the position to veto any significant evolution in the direction of an *economic* organization. At the end of the day, stalemates tend to strengthen the intergovernmental side, more than the community side, of the EU.

If it is true that the EU and the United States are op-ed polities that should be held together more by a *method* to handle disagreement than by a *model* for its resolution,[90] nevertheless a method, in order to be viable, requires the sharing of common values and criteria for waging those disputes. Spinelli would be happy to know that the EU, with the Laeken process, has finally begun to discuss the reasons for, and the nature of, integration in constitutional terms.[91]

But this constitutional debate has also made manifest the difficult conciliation between the *economic* and the *political* view of the EU. In sum, the EU needs a common document for elaborating a shared constitutional language able to frame the disputes among Europeans and for regulating them through non-unanimous procedural criteria. At the same time, those constitutional disputes are precluding the approval of such a document. How can this conundrum be resolved? One might wonder whether Spinelli would have given a new perspective on the constitutional discussion of the future, based on the recognition that the two Europes are too far apart to be reconciled in a common document, thus suggesting the need to give a differentiated constitutional basis to them (material to one and formal to the other).

Notes

1. Piero S. Graglia, *Altiero Spinelli* (Bologna: Il Mulino, 2008).

2. Comparative works on American and European experiences of integration were few till the 2000s. Among them, the most significant are certainly Mauro Cappelletti, Monica Seccombe, and Joseph. H. H. Weiler (eds.), *Integration Through Law: Europe and the American Federal Experience* (Berlin: De Gruyter), vol. 1. In the 2000s, more systematic comparative studies started to appear, among them see, Kalypso Nicolaïdis and Robert Howse, *The Federal Vision: Legitimacy and Levels of Governance in the United States and the European Union* (Oxford: Oxford University Press, 2001); David Mckay, *Designing Europe: Comparative Lessons from the Federal Experience* (Oxford: Oxford University Press, 2001); Leslie F. Goldstein, *Constituting Federal Sovereignty: The European Union in Comparative Context* (Baltimore: The Johns Hopkins University Press, 2001); Nicolas Jabko and Craig Parsons (eds.), *With US or Against US? European Trends in American Perspective* (Oxford, Oxford University Press, 2005); and Anand Menon and Martin Schain (eds.), *Comparative Federalism: The European Union and the United States in Comparative Perspective* (Oxford: Oxford University Press, 2006). All these comparative studies, however, focused exclusively on the federal organization of the United States (U.S.) and the quasi-federal organization of the EU.

3. Altiero Spinelli, "Il modello costituzionale americano e i tentativi di unità europea," in Altiero Spinelli, *Il progetto europeo* (Bologna, Il Mulino, 1985): 151–62, 157.

4. As is widely accepted, the name of European Union (EU) includes the various stages of European integration, which started with the 1957 Rome Treaty as the European Economic Community (EEC) to become, with the 1992 Maastricht Treaty, the European Union (EU). The EU is the name of a new organization structured around three pillars, the first one represented by the EEC created through the 1957 Rome Treaty. The 1997 Amsterdam Treaty thus transformed the EEC into the European Community (EC).

5. Giovanni Sartori, "Concept Misinformation and Comparative Politics," *The American Political Science Review*, 64, 4 (1970): 1033–41.

6. See Andrew Glencross, "Altiero Spinelli and the Idea of the U.S. Constitution as a Model for Europe: The Promises and Pitfalls of an Analogy," *Journal of Common Market Studies*, 47, no. 2 (2009): 287–307; Sergio Fabbrini, *Compound Democracies: Why the United States and Europe Are Becoming Similar* (Oxford: Oxford University Press, 2000).

7. To better conceptualize both the United States and EU, I tried to bring the "federal paradigm" into a larger "democratic paradigm" in several works published during the 2000s; see in particular Sergio Fabbrini, *Compound Democracies: Why the United States and Europe Are Becoming Similar* (Oxford: Oxford University Press, 2007). To me, federalism is only one defining feature of unions of states. What makes the United States and the EU (and Switzerland) different from other federal polities is their separation of powers also at the horizontal level, and not only at the vertical level. Because of a dramatic lack of comparative knowledge in EU studies, this peculiarity of asymmetrical unions of states is generally missing.

8. I am referring to the Constitutional Treaty approved by the European Council in 2004 and then rejected by the voters in a referendum held in France in May 2005 and in the Netherlands in June 2005 and thus the Lisbon Treaty, which reabsorbed a large part but not the more symbolic aspects of the CT, was finally accepted by all the 27 member states, and came into force on December 1, 2009, after prolonged contestation by the Irish voters, the Czech and Polish presidents, and the German constitutional court.

9. Giandomenico Majone, *Dilemmas of European Integration. The Ambiguities and Pitfalls of Integration by Stealth* (Oxford: Oxford University Press, 2005).

10. Fritz Scharpf, *Governing in Europe. Effective and Democratic?* (Oxford: Oxford University Press, 1999).

11. Daniel J. Elazar, "The United States and the European Union: Models of Their Epochs," in Kalypso Nicolaïdis and Robert Howse (eds.), *The Federal Vision and Levels of Governance in the U.S. and in the EU* (Oxford: Oxford University Press, 2001): 31–53.

12. Simon Hix, *The Political System of the European Union* (New York: Palgrave Macmillan, 2nd edition, 2005).

13. Arendt Lijphart, *Patterns of Democracy: Government Forms and Performance in Thirty-Six Countries* (New Haven: Yale University Press, 1999); Sergio Fabbrini, *Politica comparata. Introduzione alle democrazie contemporanee* (Roma-Bari: Laterza, 2008).

14. The concept of compoundness derives from the American debate while in Europe the concept of compoundness has been generally unknown. James Madison used it for the first time in the 1787 Philadelphia constitutional convention; see Max Farrand, *The Records of the Federal Convention of 1787* (New Haven: Yale University Press, 1966). Robert A. Dahl investigated the anti-majoritarian nature of Madisonian democracy in his *A Preface to Democratic Theory. Expanded Edition* (New Haven:

Yale University Press, 2006). Vincent Ostrom has clarified the political theory of a compound republic in *The Political Theory of a Compound Republic. Designing the American Experiment*, (Lincoln: University of Nebraska Press, 2nd revised edition, 1987). David C. Hendrickson's *Peace Pact. The Lost World of the American Founding* (Lawrence: The University Press of Kansas, 2003) has discussed the unionist paradigm of a republic of many republics which inspired (with the republican and liberal paradigms) the American founding fathers. Recently, an American scholar has used it for addressing polities characterized by a low degree of institutional centralization (such as Germany and Italy, other than the EU). See Vivien Schmidt, *Democracy in Europe. The EU and National Polities* (Oxford: Oxford University Press, 2006). In my approach, compoundness is more than a generic property of noncentralized political systems. Indeed, it is the analytical property of a democratic model characterized by a basic institutional feature: multiple separations of powers. It is an ideal-type comparable to Lijphart's ideal-types of majoritarian democracy or consensual democracy, but distinguishable from them because of that institutional feature (and thus because of the properties of the political process structured by it). For this reason, in my parsimonious approach, the compound democracy model might be applicable only to those polities organized around multiple separations of powers (such as the United States, Switzerland, and the EU). It is interesting to notice that all three of them are unions of states, although with different degrees of integration. Of course, an analytical model, or ideal-type, cannot be confused with an historical case. In fact, it is a genus to which belong different species.

15. Stefano Bartolini, *Restructuring Europe: Centre Formation, System Building, and Political Structuring Between the Nation State and the European Union* (Oxford: Oxford University Press, 2005).

16. Indeed, in the case of the Commission, a specific form of check and balance has been introduced, with the European Council nominating its members with the advice and consent of the Parliament. Although the Lisbon Treaty talks of the "election" of the Commission by the Parliament, in reality the Parliament has to approve (or to disapprove) the proposal of the European Council (and not "to elect" a Commission as domestic parliaments, or the majorities of their members, elect their governments).

17. Charlie Jeffery and Peter Savigear, *German Federalism Today* (Leicester: Leicester University Press, 1991).

18. Sergio Fabbrini, "Madison in Brussels: The EU and the U.S. as Compound Democracies," *European Political Science*, 4, no. 2 (2005): 188–98.

19. Lijphart, *Patterns of Democracy*.

20. Jon Elster, *Ways of Constitution-Making*, in A. Hadenius (ed.), *Democracy's Victory and Crisis* (Cambridge: Cambridge University Press, 1997): 123–42.

21. Daniel J. Elazar, "Constitution-Making: The Pre-eminently Political Act," in Keith G. Banting and Richard Simeon (eds.), *Redesigning the State: The Politics of Constitutional Change in Industrial Nations* (Toronto: University of Toronto Press, 1985): 232–48.

22. Both in (West) Germany and in Israel it was an explicit choice of the post Second World War ruling political elite to approve a fundamental law but not a constitution. Through that choice, the political elite wanted to underline the "transitory" nature of the political regime, because of the still Jewish diaspora (in the Israeli case) and the division between West and East (in the German case). It is interesting to notice that the 1990 *Deutsche Einheit* or "German unity" was not based on (finally) a new formal constitution. Indeed, it has coincided with the inclusion of the five eastern *Länder* into the (eleven *Länder of* the western) German federal state.

23. See Michelle Everson and Julia Eisner, *The Making of a European Constitution. Judges and Law Beyond Constitutive Power* (London: Routledge, 2007); cf. Paul Craig and Gráinne de Búrca, *The Evolution of EU Law* (Oxford: Oxford University Press, 1999); Bruno de Witte, "Direct Effect, Supremacy and the Nature of Legal Order," in Paul Craig and Gráinne de Búrca (eds.), *The Evolution of EU Law* (Oxford: Oxford University Press, 1999): 177–213.

24. Deirdre Curtin and Alfred E. Kellerman, *The EU Constitution: The Best Way Forward?* (The Hague: Asser Press, 2006).

25. Thomas Christiansen and Christine Reh, *Constitutionalizing the European Union* (New York: Palgrave Macmillan, 2009).

26. Antje Wiener, *The Invisible Constitution of Politics: Contested Norms and International Encounters* (Cambridge: Cambridge University Press, 2008), 26.

27. Berthold Rittberger and Frank Schimmelfennig (eds.), *The Constitutionalization of the European Union* (London: Routledge, 2007); Alec Stone Sweet and James Caporaso, "From Free Trade to Supranational Polity: The European Court and Integration," in W. Sandholtz and A. Stone Sweet (eds.), *European Integration and Supranational Governance* (Oxford: Oxford University Press, 1998): 92–133.

28. Michael O'Neill, *Struggle for the European Constitution: A Past and Future History* (London: Routledge, 2008); Michael Longo, *Constitutionalizing Europe: Processes and Practices* (Aldershot: Ashgate, 2006).

29. Indeed the United Kingdom, after it has moved in the direction of territorial devolution, recognizing the distinct identity of Scotland and Wales, has been forced to consider the approval of a formal document; see Desmond King, *The English Constitution* (Oxford: Oxford University Press, 2009).

30. Alec Stone Sweet, "The Constitutionalization of the EU: Steps Towards a Supranational Polity," in Sergio Fabbrini (ed.), *Democracy and Federalism in the European Union and the United States. Exploring Post-National Governance* (London: Routledge, 2005): 44–56; Alec Stone Sweet, Wayne Sandholtz and Neil Fligstein (eds.), *The Institutionalization of Europe* (Oxford: Oxford University Press, 2001).

31. Christine Reh, "The Lisbon Treaty: De-Constitutionalizing the European Union?" *Journal of Common Market Studies* 47, 3 (2009): 625–50.

32. It is possible to argue that in the case of Norway the decision not to be a member state of the EU is justified by purely economic reasons. In the case of Switzerland, however, that decision has a deeper cause. Switzerland has a difficulty in becoming a member state of the EU because this membership might jeopardize the stability of

the pact between its various linguistic/national communities. See Hans-Peter Kriesi and Alexander H. Trechsel, *The Politics of Switzerland* (Cambridge: Cambridge University Press, 2008). It is difficult for a compound democracy to become a member of another, albeit larger, compound democracy.

33. Joseph H. H. Weiler and Ulrich R. Haltern, "Constitutional or International? The Foundations of the Community Legal Order and the Question of Judicial Kompetenz-Kompetenz," in Anne-Marie Slaughter, Alec Stone Sweet and Joseph H. H. Weiler (eds.), *The European Courts and National Courts: Doctrine and Jurisprudence* (Oxford: Hart, 1998): 331–64.

34. In the following sections I further develop themes discussed in Sergio Fabbrini, "The Constitutionalisation of a Compound Democracy: Comparing the European Union with the American Experience," *ConWEB-Webpapers on Constitutionalism & Governance beyond the State- www.bath.ac.uk/esml/conWEB*, 2008, no. 3, ISSN: 1756-7556.

35. Bruce Ackerman, *We The People. Foundations* (Cambridge, Mass: Harvard University Press, 1991): 15.

36. Daniel J. Elazar, *The American Constitutional Tradition* (Lincoln: University of Nebraska Press, 1988).

37. Murray Forsyth, *Unions of States. The Theory and Practice of Confederation* (New York: Leicester University Press, 1981).

38. Hendrickson, *Peace Pact*: 7.

39. Daniel H. Deudney, *Bounding Power: Republican Security Theory From the Polis to the Global Village* (Princeton, NJ: Princeton University Press, 2007), chapter 6.

40. Nicolas Onuf and Peter Onuf, *Federal Union, Modern World. The Law of Nations in an Age of Revolutions, 1776–1814* (Madison, WI: Madison House, 1993).

41. Hendrickson, *Peace Pact*: 258.

42. Samuel Kernell (ed.), *James Madison: The Theory and Practice of Republican Government* (Stanford: Stanford University Press, 2003).

43. Vincent Ostrom, *American Federalism. Constituting a Self-Governing Society* (San Francisco: ICS Press, 1993).

44. With the sole exception of Nebraska which adopted a unicameral system in 1934.

45. Richard E. Neustadt, *Presidential Power and the Modern Presidents. The Politics of Leadership from Roosevelt to Reagan* (New York: The Free Press, 3rd edition, 1990): 27.

46. Martin Shapiro, "The Success of Judicial Review and Democracy," in Martin Shapiro and Alec Stone Sweet, *On Law, Politics and Judicialization* (Oxford: Oxford University Press): 136–48.

47. Of course, also in the European nation-states the governors are obliged to respect constitutional principles and procedures, but once they have done so they are constitutionally empowered to legislate. Such legislation may be subject to *constitutional review* exercised by a specific constitutional court and initiated by another public institution, but it is certainly not subject to a judicial review initiated

by an individual citizen and exercised by ordinary courts. On the crucial difference between constitutional review and judicial review see Alec Stone Sweet, *Governing with Judges. Constitutional Politics in Europe* (Oxford: Oxford University Press, 2000) chapters 2 and 5.

48. Theodore Lowi, *The Personal President: Power Invested Promise Unfulfilled* (Ithaca, NY: Cornell University Press, 1985).

49. Nelson W. Polsby, *How Congress Evolves: Social Bases of Institutional Change* (Oxford: Oxford University Press, 2004).

50. Charles O. Jones, *Separate But Equal Branches: Congress and the Presidency* (Chatham, MA.: Chatham House Publishers, 2nd edition, 1999).

51. Timothy J. Conlan, *From New Federalism to Devolution: Twenty-Five Years of Intergovernmental Reform* (Washington, DC: Brookings Institution Press, 1998).

52. Samuel H. Beer, *To Make a Nation. The Rediscovery of American Federalism* (Cambridge, Mass. Harvard University Press, 1993).

53. Quoted in Charles A. Beard (ed.) *The Enduring Federalist* (New York: Frederick Ungar Publishing Co., 1948), 39.

54. Andrew Glencross, *What Makes the EU Viable? European Integration in the Light of the Antebellum U.S. Experience* (New York: Palgrave Macmillan, 2009).

55. Richard F. Bensel, *Sectionalism and American Political Development: 1880–1980* (Madison: The University of Wisconsin Press, 1987).

56. Alberta Sbragia, *Debt Wish. Entrepreneurial Cities, U.S. Federalism and Economic Development* (Pittsburgh: University of Pittsburgh Press, 1996).

57. Daniel J. Elazar, *The American Mosaic: The Impact of Space, Time, and Culture on American Politics* (Boulder, Co.: Westview Press, 1994): 284.

58. Leon D. Epstein, *Political Parties in the American Mold* (Madison: The University of Wisconsin Press, 1986).

59. William M. Lunch, *The Nationalization of American Politics* (Berkeley: The University of California Press, 1987).

60. On the history of populism see Michael Kazin, *The Populist Persuasion: An American History* (New York: Basic Books, 1995).

61. Sanford Levinson (ed.), *Responding to Imperfection. The Theory and Practice of Constitutional Amendment* (Princeton: Princeton University Press, 1995).

62. The American President is elected indirectly by ad-hoc presidential electors organized in the Electoral College of each state. Each state is entitled to a number of presidential electors equal to the number of representatives plus senators that state has in Congress (thus there is no national college of presidential electors). This method of apportionment of the presidential electors obviously favors the small states over the big ones. In fact, whereas the number of representatives is proportional to the size of the population, the number of senators is not. Indeed, every state is entitled to two senators irrespective of its demographic size. Thus, through the states' Electoral College, the smaller states carry a political weight disproportionate to their population in the election of the President. See Robert A. Dahl, *How Democratic Is the American Constitution* (New Haven: Yale University Press, 2001).

63. Ackerman, *We The People*, chapter 5.

64. J. D. Greenstone, *The Lincoln Persuasion. Remaking American Liberalism* (Princeton: Princeton University Press, 1993).

65. Ackerman, *We The People*: 36.

66. Richard B. Bernstein, *Amending America. If We Love the Constitution So Much, Why Do We Keep Trying to Change It?* (Lawrence: University Press of Kansas, 1995).

67. Desmond Dinan, *Ever Closer Union: An Introduction to European Integration* (New York: Palgrave, 2005).

68. Tony Judt, *Postwar: A History of Europe since 1945* (London: Penguin, 2005).

69. On this point see David Calleo, *Rethinking Europe's Future* (Princeton: Princeton University Press, 2001) and G. John Ikenberry, *After Victory: Institutions, Strategic Restraints and the Rebuilding of Order after Major Wars* (Princeton: Princeton University Press, 2000).

70. David Hendrickson, "Of Power and Providence," *Policy Review*, 135 (2006): 1–10.

71. See Dahl, *A Preface to Democratic Theory*.

72. Leon Lindberg, *The Political Dynamics of European Economic Integration* (Stanford: Stanford University Press, 1963).

73. Stephan Stetter, *EU Foreign and Interior Policies. Cross-Pillar Politics and the Social Construction of Sovereignty* (London: Routledge, 2007); cf. Armin von Bogdandy, "The European Union as a Supranational Federation: A Conceptual Attempt in Light of the Amsterdam Treaty," *Columbia Journal of European Law*, 6, 1 (Winter 2000): 27–54.

74. I am referring to the *Treaty establishing a Constitution for Europe*. It was signed on 29 October 2004, in Rome, by representatives of the then 25 member states of the EU and was subject to ratification by all member states. Its main aims were to replace the overlapping set of existing treaties that compose the EU, to codify fundamental rights throughout the EU and clarify its institutional system. For the full story behind this project see Peter Norman, *The Accidental Constitution. The Story of the European Convention* (Brussels, Eurocomment, 2003) and Bruno de Witte (ed.), *Ten Reflections on the Constitutional Treaty for Europe* (Florence: Robert Schuman Centre for Advanced Studies, 2003).

75. Neil Walker, "The EU as a Constitutional Project," *Federal Trust Online Papers* (April 2004).

76. Jo Shaw, "What Happens if the Constitutional Treaty is Not Ratified?" in Ingolf Pernice and Jiri Zemaneck (eds.), *The Treaty on a Constitution for Europe: Perspectives after the IGC* (Baden-Baden: Nomos, 2005).

77. Formally the Lisbon Treaty refers to the *Treaty amending the Treaty on European Union and the Treaty Establishing the European Community*, thereby referring both to the Treaty on European Union (TEU, Maastricht 1992) and the Treaty establishing the European Community (TEC, Rome 1957), the latter renamed *Treaty on the Functioning of the European Union* (TFEU) (Council of the European Union, 2007). The two consolidated treaties would form the legal basis of the EU (with the Charter of

Fundamental Rights). Prominent changes in the Lisbon Treaty include the scrapping of the pillar system, reduced paralysis in the Council of Ministers due to the use of qualified majority voting for an increased number of policies, a more powerful European Parliament through extended co-decision with the EU Council, as well as new tools for greater coherence and continuity in external policies, such as a long-term President of the European Council and a High Representative for Foreign Affairs.

78. Alberta Sbragia *et al.*, "Symposium: The EU and its 'Constitution'," *PS: Political Science and Politics*, XXXIX, 2 (2006): 237–72.

79. Paul Magnette and Kalypso Nicolaïdis, "Coping with the Lilliput Syndrome: Large vs. Small States in the European Convention," *Politique Européenne*, 14 (2004): 1–25.

80. Andrew Geddes, *The European and British Politics* (New York: Palgrave, 2004).

81. Neil MacCormick, "Liberalism, Nationalism and the Post-Sovereign State," in Richard Bellamy and Dario Castiglione (eds.), *Constitutionalism in Transformation: European and Theoretical Perspectives* (Oxford: Blackwell, 1996): 141–55.

82. See Charles Tilly (ed.), *The Formation of National States in Western Europe* (Princeton: Princeton University Press, 1975).

83. Alain Guyomarch, Howard Machin, and Ella Ritchie (eds.), *France in the European Union* (New York: Palgrave Macmillan, 1998).

84. Timothy Garton Ash, *Free World: America, Europe and the Surprising Future of the West* (New York: Random House, 2004).

85. Paul Taggart, "The Domestic Politics of the 2005 French and Dutch Referendums and Their Challenge for the Study of European Integration," *Journal of Common Market Studies*, 44 (2006 Annual Review): 7–25.

86. Paul Pierson, "Increasing Returns, Path Dependency and the Study of Politics," *American Political Science Review*, 94, 2 (2000): 251–67.

87. Mario Monti, "Referendum: *Quid Agendum*? Réflexions pour sortir l'UE de la paralysie assurée," contribution to the "Etats généraux de l'Europe," Lyon, June 20, 2008.

88. See Spinelli, "Il modello costituzionale americano."

89. Miguel Maduro, "Europe and the Constitution: What If This is as Good as It Gets?" in Marlene Wind and Joseph H. Weiler (eds.), *Constitutionalism beyond the State* (Cambridge: Cambridge University Press, 2003): 74–102.

90. Sergio Fabbrini, *America and Its Critics. Virtues and Vices of the Democratic Hyperpower* (Cambridge: Polity Press, 2008).

91. For different perspectives on this process see Neil Walker, "After Finalité? The Future of the European Constitutional Idea," European University Institute Law Department Working Paper (Florence, 2007); Erik Eriksen, John Fossum and Augustin J. Menéndez (eds.), *Developing a Constitution for Europe* (London: Routledge, 2004); Bruno de Witte, "The Closest Thing to a Constitutional Conversation in Europe: The Semi-Permanent Treaty Revision Process," in Paul Beaumont, Carol Lyons and Neil Walker (eds.), *Convergence and Divergence in European Public Law* (Oxford: Hart, 2002): 39–57.

CHAPTER FOUR

Altiero Spinelli and the Idea of the U.S. Constitution as a Model for Europe

The Promises and Pitfalls of an Analogy

Andrew Glencross

In a 1957 essay entitled *Il modello costituzionale americano e i tentavi di unità europea* Altiero Spinelli explored the validity of seeking inspiration from the U.S. constitutional experience to devise the institutional architecture of European integration. Spinelli's essay was entirely in keeping with the twin axes of his lifelong practical and theoretical engagement with the project of European unity: it criticized the functionalist approach and advocated instead the need for a constitutional foundation for the pooling of sovereignty. This chapter uses Spinelli's essay as a point of departure for assessing the promises and pitfalls of the analogy he developed—one which is proving increasingly popular today—between the predicament of European integration and the constitutional politics of the U.S. republic. In particular, the analysis focuses on the fundamentally interrelated issues of the organization of sovereignty and arrangements for ensuring democratic accountability.

The chapter is structured as follows. The first section reviews Spinelli's attempt to draw lessons for European integration from the U.S. constitutional founding. The second section scrutinizes Spinelli's key assumption that by choosing the constitutional avenue the U.S. founding resolved the twofold problem of sovereignty clashes and democratic restraint of federal power. Section three reviews the EU experience of handling problems of sovereignty and democracy within a functionalist framework that Spinelli saw as the dreaded rival to a constitutional model based on the U.S. experience.

Finally, the fourth section explores what can be learnt from the transatlantic comparison, especially with reference to the various projects of EU democratization debated in the context of the enduring constitutional crisis sparked off by the defunct Constitutional Treaty. A concluding section closes the argument.

Spinelli's Contrast between the Constitutional and the Functionalist Model of European Unity: Two Perspectives on the U.S. Analogy

Spinelli believed that functionalists and federalists were at odds in their appreciation of the validity of drawing on the U.S. constitutional model when designing the institutions of European integration. According to this interpretation, functionalists rejected the pertinence of the analogy because the various conditions for a viable federal constitution (similar economic development, linguistic and cultural homogeneity, and little experience as independent sovereign units) were not present in the European case. Nonetheless, the analogy remained germane from a longer-term functionalist perspective: "federation had to be the endpoint and not the starting point of the process of [European] unification, unlike what occurred in the United States."[1] In this sense the ultimate goal of functionalism was beholden to the U.S. model even if the process of reaching this constitutional conclusion was to take a different course.

Conversely, European federalists, like Spinelli himself of course, sought to draw immediate inspiration from the U.S. federal model in their quest to reorganize political authority in Europe. For Spinelli this claim was partly based on a historical argument that functionalists were deceived in thinking that the constitutional success of the U.S. federal experiment was due to propitious historical circumstances. This auspicious interpretation of the origins of the U.S. Constitution was, he pointed out, belied by the far from sanguine assessments of the future of American unity voiced by many commentators in the period of the Philadelphia Convention. Moreover, functionalists conveniently overlooked the fact that U.S. federalism had a highly credible rival form of political organization, the confederal model, which in the debates over the proposed constitution was often taken to be the appropriate arrangement of sovereignty for the former British colonies. As Spinelli rightly recalled, in the 1780s many political actors "dared not think it possible to go beyond the model of a confederation of sovereign states."[2]

Spinelli, however, did not simply seek to refute the Whig-like interpretation of the supposed "pre-conditions" for a successful federal constitution.

His fondness for the U.S. analogy was also linked to the conceptual premise that the U.S. Constitution was designed as a solution to problems of sovereignty and democracy identical to those facing European states in the postwar context. It was precisely this commonality that Spinelli identified as the fundamental reason why Europe had much to learn from the U.S. model of federal constitutionalism. Thus he remarked that "the supranational unification of certain specific aspects of public authority cannot escape the logic of the U.S. system, because they both belong to the same logic of the construction of political authority."[3] Hence the importance of the U.S. analogy for the European case lies in the fact that they both faced the "same problem of the establishment of political authority and the specification of its limits."[4]

Spinelli thus characterized the U.S. federal constitution of 1789 as a system for creating a sovereign power "whose capacity to decide and execute would be independent of the goodwill of the single states, because these latter would ordinarily be competent to administer public affairs only as they pertained to their particular community."[5] Identical to the U.S. constitutional doctrine of federalism as a system of "dual federalism,"[6] in Spinelli's essay this interpretation implied that "state and federation would each have in common, on the one hand, the citizen, belonging equally to the state and the federation, obliged to obey the laws of both and owing taxes to both, and, on the other hand, state and federation would each have a common duty to obey a federal court whose task was to uphold the federal pact, deciding whether one or the other power had acted beyond its competences and invaded those of the other."[7]

Furthermore, beyond the problem of sovereignty, the constitution was also intended to conserve democratic accountability at each level by "guaranteeing both the various elements of the separation of powers and the control of the governed over the governing."[8] European federalists, in their struggle against the functionalist logic of integration, thus confronted the same constitutional predicament as that of the U.S. founding fathers, namely: "what kind of European political authority should exercise what competences and how should these be established?"[9]

Spinelli thus used the U.S. experience to advocate the need for a similar constitutional, rather than functionalist, blueprint for European integration. The argument, therefore, is fully in keeping with his strategy to convoke a European constituent assembly modeled on the Philadelphia Convention to produce such a constitutional outcome. However, this chapter does not seek to question the validity of the constituent assembly approach to the problem of European integration, which in any case has already attracted serious academic interest largely thanks to Europe's own attempt to mimic

Philadelphia, the Convention on the Future of Europe. Rather, I propose to examine the central supposition underlying Spinelli's general argument about why the U.S. constitutional model is so relevant for the European integration project. Namely, the claim that the U.S. Constitution, which has survived to become the oldest republican founding document in existence, from the outset resolved certain crucial problems of sovereignty and democracy. It is this supposition that needs to be scrutinized in order to assess exactly the merits and demerits of making an analogy with the U.S. founding when discussing the reorganization of political authority in Europe. It is hoped that such an analysis will nuance Spinelli's argument about what European integration can learn from the U.S. model, so as to turn the analogy into less of a nostrum and more of a tool for critical reflection on the nature of constitutional issues in the EU.

To What Extent Did the U.S. Constitution Resolve Issues of State Sovereignty and Popular Sovereignty?

The U.S. constitutional founding did not specify a single locus of sovereignty. In this way, the constitution symbolized the retention of the Tudor principle of a government of "separated institutions sharing powers,"[10] which the colonists had fought to preserve in the face of the new-fangled British doctrine of parliamentary sovereignty. Dual federalism, the sharing of powers between state and federal level, consists of four features: "The national government is one of enumerated powers only; the purposes which it may constitutionally promote are few; within their respective spheres the two centers of government are "sovereign" and hence "equal"; the relation of the two centers to each other is one of tension rather than collaboration."[11]

The establishment of two sovereign centers of government in tension with each other meant that from the outset the Supreme Court was expected to be the arbiter in the predicted struggles over jurisdictional competence. Certainly this was the intention of Publius, who wrote in *Federalist* 22 that "all nations have found it necessary to establish one court paramount to the rest, possessing a general superintendence, and authorized to settle and declare in the last resort a uniform rule of civil justice."[12] This explains why Spinelli felt inspired by what he saw as the U.S. constitutional model's institutional ability to settle issues of competing sovereignty claims by establishing a pellucid competence catalogue (albeit with the possibility of constitutional amendment) overseen by a supreme tribunal.

However, the record of clashing sovereignty claims after the U.S. Constitution came into force in 1789 is far more complex, involving as well as affecting the exercise of popular sovereignty. Simply put, U.S. political development in the antebellum period was punctuated by a series of clashes that called into question the stability of dual federalism and the ability of the Supreme Court to resolve these federal crises. Indeed, the establishment of a federal political authority and the organization of a complex "compound" method of checking the exercise of this power heralded the birth of U.S. constitutional politics. *Pace* Spinelli, both the political authority of the federal government and the democratic means for checking its action were subject to repeated contestation.

Although this is an abstruse story, I propose to illustrate this process of contesting federal sovereignty and arguing over popular sovereignty with only a selected few examples. The chosen constitutional disputes represent clashes between different conceptions of the proper nature of the federal system, chiefly the distribution of competences and the institutionalization of popular sovereignty within the federal architecture. In this sense they are a continuation of the original federalist debates over the constitution,[13] especially since the abandonment of the Virginia plan and its proposed federal veto over state legislation left the relationship between units and union highly uncertain. The analysis will thus focus largely on the antebellum period since this was the period in which the experiment in dual sovereignty unraveled as advocates of state sovereignty clashed with nationalists over the coexistence of popular sovereignty at two levels.

The clearest examples of early struggles to define the nature of the U.S. federal system are the nullification crises of 1798 and 1832. The former concerned the so-called Alien and Sedition Acts' restriction of civil liberties, while the latter was the result of South Carolina's hostility to the imposition of tariffs on imports of manufactured goods. In the first case, two states challenged the federal government's constitutional right both to claim jurisdiction over resident aliens in a state and to restrict the liberty of the press. Under the constitution of 1789 no specific power had been granted to the federal government concerning aliens except with regard to laws of naturalization, while the bill of rights specifically protected free speech. In these circumstances the state legislatures of Kentucky and Virginia upheld the right not to comply with these federal laws, claiming in effect a veto over this unconstitutional extension of federal sovereignty, and publicized their struggle to gain the support of other state.[14] In other words, when confronted with federal legislation they deemed unconstitutional, Kentucky and Virginia found the existing system for checking federal authority wanting and thus sought a new mechanism for stymieing the exercise of federal power. Thus, less than a decade after the entry into force of the constitution, the mechanism for maintaining the distribution of sovereignty within the dual federal arrangement was already called into question.

A near-identical situation arose in 1832 over Congress' protectionist tariff on manufactured imports, which South Carolina thought unfairly targeted plantation states. The tariff crisis also marked a turning point in the antebellum period by sparking a full-blown theoretical reflection on the connection between state sovereignty and popular sovereignty within the union. South Carolina's assertion of the right to judge the constitutional limits of federal government provoked a fervent debate over whether the Union was a treaty-like compact between sovereign states or the constitution of a single people.

Opponents of South Carolina's "compact" reading of the American union pointed to the constitution's ratification by the people in separate state conventions to undermine this claim that states could unilaterally defy the federal government.[15] Hence Andrew Jackson, in his presidential proclamation on the tariff crisis, argued that the use of state conventions "show [the constitution] to be a government in which the people of all the states collectively are represented."[16] Moreover, given crucial changes affecting the presidential election such as the easing of property requirements for voting and the introduction of direct election for presidential electors, Jackson went so far as to argue that "[w]e are ONE PEOPLE in the choice of the President and Vice President. . . . The people, then, and not the States, are represented in the executive branch."[17]

It was precisely this Jacksonian innovation, whereby the presidency became a populist, national institution attenuating the original state- and elite-dominated election process—a shift further aided by the unexpected development and entrenchment of the national party system—that led to John C. Calhoun's attempt to rethink the Union. Calhoun fundamentally "thought that it was essential to revise republican theory and constitutional arrangements to fit these new circumstances."[18] The American union had to adapt to a novel situation in which despite the size of the republic and the founders' constitutional devices the federal government was now potentially the instrument of a partisan majority, especially over the slavery question. In his mind, therefore, the federal system needed remodeling in order to simultaneously resolve the outstanding question of residual state sovereignty and the proper role of popular sovereignty within this framework.

As well as delivering the definitive compact interpretation of the constitution, he developed not only a theory of "concurrent majorities" as the cornerstone of federalism but also proposed a system of nullification as an *ex post* device to counterbalance the development of a system of representation more centralized and majoritarian than at its origin. Both nullification and the notion of concurrent majorities were designed as means of using popular sovereignty at the state level to check federal authority. Reading the constitution as a compact between states meant that popular sovereignty ought to be exercised at the state rather than federal level.

The Union's victory in the Civil War was the death knell for Calhoun's compact reading of the constitution and with it the doctrines of nullification and secession: the union was the government of a single sovereign people. By virtue of its victory, the postwar Union thus acquired a new settlement as far as competency over competences was concerned. States lost their claim to be able to withdraw from the Union, nullify laws or unilaterally question the constitutionality of its acts. Under this new understanding of the constitution, therefore, popular sovereignty at the state level could not be used to unilaterally contest federal authority. However, problems of democratic accountability at the federal level were only just beginning to emerge. Even if the principle of locating popular sovereignty at the federal level had been won there remained three unanswered questions. Firstly, who was a member of the sovereign body of citizens, secondly how would it exercise its will and, thirdly, what competences could the federal government claim as a result of a popular mandate?

These problems were already apparent during Reconstruction with the stillborn civil rights movement leading to the fourteenth and fifteenth amendments that tried to emancipate former slaves. It was the Compromise of 1877, which secured the Southern Democrats' support for Republican candidate Hayes in the Presidential election, that effectively sanctioned the federal government's willingness to turn a blind eye to civil rights abuses in the former slave states, an arrangement that was to last until the 1950s. Yet civil rights—the first unresolved question, that of inclusion within the sovereign people—was only one aspect of the contestation over popular sovereignty at the federal level in the post bellum republic.

Before the second wave of civil rights activism, the federal system underwent two further defining moments in the struggle over the nature of popular sovereignty within the federal framework: the Progressive era, which led to the constitutional amendment providing for the direct election of senators in 1913, and Roosevelt's New Deal. The move from indirect to direct representation in the Senate and the contemporaneous amendment establishing a federal income tax further underlined the fact that the union was based on a single sovereign people with an unmediated connection between the individual and the federal government. Progressivism thus resolved the second question of how the sovereign body of citizens would exercise its will. It did this by ensuring that popular sovereignty at the federal level would be based on the direct participation of citizens, who would also have a greater influence over the national parties thanks to the innovation of the primaries.

Furthermore, these two moments, Progressivism and the New Deal, were in a sense complementary. While the progressive movement aimed to shake up corrupt machine politics and aloof party leaders for the sake of more responsive federal government, the New Deal conflict over the role of the judiciary was designed to prevent Supreme Court justices fettering the will of a popularly elected government. Hence the evolving nature of popular sovereignty at the federal level led to a clash with the judicial power—the third unresolved problem. This was because the Supreme Court, for a variety of reasons, remained wedded to a static concept of U.S. federalism—what Lowi has called a minimalist, "patronage state"[19]—and was prepared to uphold this even in the face of a popular mandate for greater federal intervention in the economic sphere. As a result of Roosevelt's threat to pack the Court with pliable appointees, federal competences expanded greatly, just as they also did during the later civil rights period. In this way, the twentieth-century democratization of the federal republic gave rise to new clashes over the proper scope of federal government even after the Civil War had rendered unilateral attempts to assert state sovereignty unthinkable.

This section sketched the manifold ways in which the U.S. Constitution was, over the course of more than one hundred and fifty years, beset by the twofold problem of state sovereignty and popular sovereignty. These conflicts lasted even in the face of the continuous rise of national sentiment as a result of participation in war, the expanding frontier and the birth of American literary and cultural production. Contrary to Spinelli's argument, therefore, the constitution itself did not mark the establishment of political authority and the specification of its limits once and for all. Rather, the basic rules of the game of politics were challenged repeatedly until state sovereignty withered after the Civil War, and once the New Deal—as well as the later Civil Rights movement—affirmed that federal government could use its sovereignty claim to carry out a popular mandate of competence expansion. It is now necessary to examine how Europe, which Spinelli understood to have embarked on a functionalist alternative to a constitutional federal system, has fared in handling analogous problems.

The European Experience of Sovereignty Clashes and the Problematic Institutionalization of Popular Sovereignty

The intention here is not to dispute Spinelli's claim that the functionalist avenue of integration—at least as far as he understood the concept—was pursued by contrast with the constitutional approach. Instead, the chapter explores what, if anything, this nonconstitutional method entailed for clashes of state sovereignty and the institutionalization of popular sovereignty within the architecture of integration. Again, this is a highly convoluted tale since the integration process has been addled by conflicts over competences and the problem of defining the proper relationship between member states and the EU for the purposes of democratically checking the latter. Hence the analysis focuses on the difficulties that have arisen when both these issues of state sovereignty and popular sovereignty have fused in the politics of integration.

In fact, the politics of integration have in many ways been transformed into constitutional politics *tout court* thanks to the actions of the European Court of Justice. This process of surreptitious—at least from some of the member states' perspective—constitutionalization is the result of the landmark supremacy and direct effect rulings. It is further illustrated by the Court's willingness to use the language of fundamental rights well before the Charter of Fundamental Rights was conceived.[20] Spinelli, in his attack on the functionalist nature of the EEC regime, did not anticipate how the Court's use of the preliminary reference procedure combined with the prerogative to interpret provisions of the treaty would be turned against member state sovereignty. He was not alone, since the member states expected the court to deal with disputes arising under Articles 169 and 170, which enabled the Commission or a member state, respectively, to bring a suit for a state's failure to fulfill treaty obligations. However, for present purposes, constitutionalization via law is most important for the way in which it both *changed member state expectations about the nature of integration* and *has remained only indirectly linked with popular sovereignty*.

By winning the struggle over the supremacy of European treaties and legislation and their ability to create judiciable rights for individuals against member state—neither of which existed under the ECSC treaty—the Court clearly distinguished the EEC from an ordinary international organization. In fact, the authors of *The Federalist* would have immediately recognized the import of these changes since Publius identified "the characteristic difference between a league and a government" as precisely the ability to "extend the authority of the Union to the persons of the citizens."[21] Member states have reacted accordingly, at least when new European policies and competences were tabled. First of all, recalcitrant countries have successfully obtained opt-outs from certain policies (notably the Euro, in the case of Denmark, Sweden, and the United Kingdom)[22] as well as specific treaty provisions shielding them from certain obligations (Denmark and Malta can maintain restrictions on nonresident home ownership, the United Kingdom is currently seeking opt-outs from being bound by the Charter of Fundamental Rights). Moreover, at Maastricht, the member states deliberately designed the pillar system so as to insulate these new areas of putative EU competence from the process of constitutionalization through law.

In restricting the jurisdiction of the ECJ over second and third pillar policy areas, the states ensured that legal acts bind states in what Publius called their "corporate or collective capacities"[23] and do not create rights for individuals. Even though the EU Constitution proposed the abolition of the pillar system, the circumscription of ECJ jurisdiction was to be maintained (Articles III-376 and III-377). A precedent for such a move can be found in the Amsterdam Treaty, where elements of the former Justice and Home Affairs pillar were integrated into the first pillar although the procedures for legislating in this area did not follow orthodox community law. The insistence on unanimity, member state co-power of initiative and reduced ECJ jurisdiction, has resulted in what has been described as the creation of a new hybrid, "intergovernmentalized EC law."[24] Indeed, this move has given rise to a new inter-institutional sovereignty game as the Commission and Council clash over which legal regime relevant legislation should fall under.

In all these instances, the justification for opting out of policies or restricting further constitutionalization to the detriment of state sovereignty has ultimately revolved around respecting the democratic legitimacy of the nation-states in the EU system. The claim that popular sovereignty rightly pertains to the national level, which alone can sanction changes to the EU system, has thus been used in a Calhounian fashion to defend state sovereignty against the threat, whether by diplomatically-negotiated treaty reform or through jurisprudence, of overweening EU competence expansion. This claim is made most explicit when opt-outs have been specifically linked to concrete manifestations of popular sovereignty at the national level. For instance, in 2003, when Sweden held a referendum on the single currency even though when it joined the EU in 1995 no formal single currency opt-out had been secured.

The ultimate logic of this claim about the many sovereigns of the EU compact was reached with the decision to introduce an explicit right of withdrawal from the EU, as specified by Article 35 of the Lisbon Treaty. How important this provision will be in practice cannot be prophesied, but it does send a clear signal about the simultaneous—what Madison would have called "compound"—confederal (treaty-based) and federal (constitutionalized) character of the EU. Hence the dual character of political representation in the EU, whereby states and their citizens are represented as separate collective entities in the Council, while individual citizens are represented as a European whole by the Parliament and Commission. The central tension between these two principles of political representation has yet to be resolved.

Another good example of the complex interplay between defining the proper locus of popular sovereignty within the EU system and retaining residual member state competences can be seen in the disputes over the introduction of further QMV or increasing the purview of the European Parliament. Both these proposals were enshrined in the so-called Spinelli Draft Treaty Establishing the European Union (1984) and have since remained a core belief among Euro-enthusiasts. In particular, as Fabbrini has noted, it is commonly assumed "that the parliamentary model is the only viable solution to the question of the democratization of the EU."[25] In an attenuated form, the parliamentarization of the EU has occurred thanks to the introduction of co-decision; the use of QMV has also been extended. However, member states have likewise been adamant in their unwillingness to countenance either the wholesale generalization of QMV or the extension of co-decision to all policy fields, thereby perpetuating the antagonistic co-existence between confederal (intergovernmental) and federal (supranational) principles. Constitutionalism via the construction of supranational legal has thus not been matched by the establishment of a supranational form of popular sovereignty.

The retention of these confederal elements is justified precisely on the basis that EU policy making can—in the absence of a single European popular sovereign—only be legitimized indirectly by the democratically elected member state governments that participate in EU decision making. Another way of putting this is that the member states can collectively decide to delegate some of their sovereign authority for specific ends without thereby creating a superior locus of sovereignty to be made accountable to a single community. Nonetheless, constitutionalism implies the limitation of member state sovereignty, even in policy areas lacking formal EU competence, as in the recent case where the ECJ frustrated Austrian attempts to restrict the number of German students entering its university system. In fact, the anticipated impact of unwanted constitutionalism is the motivating force behind the United Kingdom's opt out of the provisions of the Charter of Fundamental rights.

Unsurprisingly, the opaque and ambiguous EU political system that has been established as a result of the awkward juxtaposition of constitutionalism and intergovernmentalism has provoked a critical reexamination of the norms of democracy itself. In particular, a serious attempt has been made to shift the notion of democratic accountability away from the paradigm of popular sovereignty and representative government. This explains the use of terms such as "pluralist democracy"[26] and "audit democracy"[27] alongside the development of proxies for constituting democracy such as democratic governance[28] or "limited democratic politics."[29] None of these alternative conceptions of democracy, however, has proved capable of sundering the link with popular sovereignty, which explains why the EU is still beset by democratic deficit anxiety.

The newest element in this tussle over the nature of state sovereignty and the exercise of popular sovereignty within the EU concerns the use of referendums to ratify treaty reform in certain member states. Referendums were intended to act as improved—compared with indirect legitimacy via national governments—legitimating devices to connect the multiple popular sovereigns of the EU with the project of deeper integration. Ironically, the referendum experience has instead revealed the glaring gap, in many member states, between political elites and citizens over integration issues,[30] thereby leading some to question the very legitimacy of holding referendums on treaty matters.

Here again the issue of popular sovereignty intersects with the problem of member states' competence claims since the denial of a state's right to hold a referendum is obviously an abrogation of its competences. Although referendums on treaty matters have existed since the 1970s (a decade in which France voted on enlargement and the United Kingdom chose to remain in the EEC) and have even failed in the recent past (in Denmark in 1992, in Ireland in 2001) it is the scuppering of the EU Constitution by popular votes in France and the Netherlands that has led to a thorough questioning of the appropriateness of this method of ratification. On the one hand, some have used this crisis to denounce any resort to the referendum device for treaty reform, while others have looked to the Swiss experience to recommend the introduction of Europe-wide referendums with a double majority of citizens and states. Thus the former approach calls for the end of national referendums on EU treaties whereas the latter approves their use so long as they cannot become tantamount to national vetoes. Only Philippe Schmitter has dared to suggest that simultaneous national treaty referendums could be used creatively to determine the contours of EU constitutionalism by allowing certain member states to plump for greater integration more while leaving others in a looser confederative association. Grasping the inherent connection between popular sovereignty and competence issues, Schmitter seeks to use the former to settle the latter—a novel method of escaping the unanimity trap for EU treaty reform.[31]

The referendum issue, therefore, has merely complicated the twofold problem of sovereignty clashes and the institutionalization of popular sovereignty. In terms of state competences, the establishment of EU supremacy and direct effect has had an unequivocal impact on determining the scope of member state sovereignty. Yet within the constitutional politics of the EU this settlement remains the exception,[32] while the problem of the nature and exercise of popular sovereignty has become more vexing. In the light of this analysis, the next section reviews the appropriateness of drawing comparisons with the United States and comments on the validity of Spinelli's own transatlantic analogy.

Promises and Pitfalls of the EU/U.S. Analogy

Bringing together the analysis of both political systems from the previous two sections reveals that some of Spinelli's implicit assumptions about why the U.S. Constitution could serve as a model for European integration were misguided. First of all, it should be evident that he overstated the importance of the U.S. constitutional foundation when it came to "the establishment of political authority and the specification of its limits."[33] The course of political development charted above only confirms Lowi's pithy remark that "the United States of 1789 was neither united nor a state."[34] The authority of the U.S. government and the means for limiting its functioning were subject to repeated contestation in ways not imagined by Spinelli, for whom the U.S. Constitution could be resumed to the states' and federal government's "common duty to obey a federal court whose task was to uphold the federal pact."[35] When this contestation reached its paroxysm, the United States experienced a series of new constitutional foundations, the Civil War, the New Deal, and Civil Rights.[36]

Moreover, the constitutional road not taken by Europe appears not to have made a significant difference to the nature of the debates over state sovereignty and the institutionalization of popular sovereignty when compared to the U.S. experience. The analysis has shown that despite its so-called functional origins, the integration process has nonetheless been confronted by constitutional disputes analogous to those occurring in the course of U.S. political development. Functionalism was thus no bar to the rise of constitutional politics in Europe. Hence the value of the analogy seems to reside neither in taking the U.S. Constitution as a template for immediate constitutional change nor as a blueprint for eventual full EU constitutionalization. Rather, the comparison is most useful in that it reveals the shared struggles to institutionalize popular sovereignty as a way of checking the limits of federal authority.

This was not something Spinelli seems to have considered troublesome in the U.S. case as he simply stated that "the Americans, like today's Europeans, desired to be ruled only by a democratic exercise of power."[37] Yet as was shown above, the practice of popular sovereignty was a deeply divisive issue, giving rise to more than simply Calhoun's attempt to disprove the Jacksonian notion of the single sovereign people. Other features of this struggle include the decades of repression in the racist South over blacks' inclusion in the sovereign body, the Progressive movement's successful campaign for direct representation of citizens in the federal Senate and the New Deal clash between popular sovereignty and judicial authority. The result was that constitutionalism eventually came to be complemented by the institutionalization of popular sovereignty at the federal level.

The contrast with Europe on this point is significant. Direct representation was achieved in 1979 with the first elections to the EP, even if the EU is far from a fully parliamentary regime. This change in the institutional architecture further complicated the mixture of confederal and federal principles of representation by creating a body that can claim to represent the democratic will of all Europe's citizens. With the Commission and the Court already standing for the general European interest, it is the Council of Ministers and the European Council that represent the popular sovereignty and interests of the constituent units. The result is a mixed system of government in which the checks on the exercise of political authority at the EU level arise as a result of jurisdictional turf wars. Consequently, as Majone explains, the business of government is "less in making policy for the entire polity than in questions of privileges and rights."[38] Hence the EU system, Majone convincingly argues, ought not to be mistaken for a straightforward separation of powers arrangement, based on the functional differentiation of government, as is often assumed in the comparative federalism literature.

The EU thus appears mired in a Calhounian situation—reminiscent of the antebellum republic and its constitutionalism only indirectly linked to popular sovereignty—in which the invidious question of competence attribution cannot be disentangled from the equally vexing one of institutionalizing democratic accountability via popular sovereignty. The acknowledged existence of multiple sovereigns within the EU system, as testified by the withdrawal mechanism as well as vetoes on treaty reform or enlargement, gives rise to a complex, antagonistic relationship between the exercise of popular sovereignty at the national level and European governance. So far, suggestions for the democratization of the EU have responded to this dual problematic of state sovereignty and popular sovereignty by seeking to attenuate the exercise of popular sovereignty at the national level, with few noticeable results. The mooted solution is either to shift toward a single European popular sovereign by parliamentarizing the system and abolishing vetoes as well as unilateral national referendums on treaties, or else it is to devise a system of accountability that does not rely on the exercise of popular sovereignty.

Most recently, the EU clearly attempted to go down the path of a constituent assembly *à la* Philadelphia for the sake of producing a constitutional moment to serve as proof that EU citizens could constitute a single sovereign entity. The fact that this whole exercise was unraveled by the use of popular sovereignty at the national level does not mean that referendums ought to be considered a bogey figure for integration. Building on Schmitter's intuition, rather than declaiming against their use, referendums could instead be seen as devices for defining the distribution of competences, decision-making procedures and even policies citizens of particular member states are willing to accept.

It is precisely in this context that the analogy with the United States might become more pertinent from the perspective of the road not taken. Instead of focusing on the founding document, it seems appropriate also to examine the constitutional mechanisms Calhoun envisaged for making federal government more responsive to popular sovereignty exercised at the state level. To some extent this has already been done by Schmitter, who draws on the theory of concurrent majorities to propose a redesign of the voting system in the Council.[39] However, Calhoun was also known as the theorist of the nullification device by which unilateral state nullification of federal legislation would trigger a convention of all the states to settle, by a three-quarters majority, whether a disputed law was constitutional. The nullification mechanism thus circumvented the Supreme Court—deemed biased toward federal self-aggrandizement—for judging issues of constitutional authority and denied the federal government the right to interpret the limits of its own authority.

Instead of being simply a unit veto, therefore, nullification was a means to engender constitutional debate about competences between, on the one hand, states and their citizens and, on the other, the states and the federal government—a dialogue not otherwise possible and one which is also vital for the EU. In fact, seeking inspiration from this moment in U.S. constitutional history appears especially germane given recent calls to increase the confederal element within the treaty system and attempts to conceptualize the EU as a *demoicracy* explicitly founded on multiple sovereigns. The Lisbon Treaty's proposal to revise the subsidiarity mechanism by incorporating national parliaments into the procedure also suggests the relevance of exploring new devices for linking the exercise of popular sovereignty at the national level with EU governance.

Conclusion

The aim of this chapter was to use Spinelli's essay on the U.S. constitutional model as the starting point for a comparative analysis of America and Europe's respective constitutional experiences. America's constitutional foundation was undoubtedly one of the major sources of inspiration for Spinelli's Euro-federalism. Although he did not seek to replicate its exact institutional framework or competence catalogue—he believed that every federal arrangement differed in this respect—the idea of a fully-fledged constitutional foundation for Europe remained his political lode star.

Yet a closer inspection of his assumptions about the U.S. constitutional model revealed the extent to which he incorrectly believed the constitution had foreclosed constitutional conflict. In particular, the twin issues of state sovereignty and the institutionalization of popular sovereignty posed serious problems for the stability and functioning of the Union. Moreover, Spinelli's jeremiad against the functionalist nature of the EEC did not anticipate the fundamental constitutional transformation that occurred within the treaty framework. Thus, despite the lack of an original constitutional moment, European integration has in fact encountered constitutional conflicts over state sovereignty and popular sovereignty similar to those arising in the course of U.S. political development.

On the one hand, therefore, the transatlantic analogy does not seem to warrant the hopes of Spinelli (and others) that a constitutional foundation will clarify and constrict the struggle over the rules of the game of integration politics. U.S. political development clearly presents a different story, one where the units disputed the authority of the union for many decades owing to their belief in keeping the locus of popular sovereignty at the state level. Even once the troublesome features of state sovereignty (secession and nullification) had been resolved in favor of the federal government, there remained unanswered questions crucial for democratic accountability: inclusion, representation, and the federal competences that could be exercised with a popular mandate.

On the other hand, the travails of the U.S. experience also suggest that the obsession with the succession of EU crises is perhaps overwrought. This is not to quibble with the serious problems of democratic legitimacy that have bedeviled the functioning of the EU. Indeed, the comparison with the United States revealed just how difficult it was to settle the issue of competence alongside democratic accountability in a compound polity. In the EU context, the recent referendums on the EU Constitution have crystallized the issue of reconciling popular sovereignty at the national level with EU-wide treaty reform. These votes triggered a reaction against referendums on treaties or at least their unilateral use. However, the analogy with the United States suggests that challenging state sovereignty directly—such as a peremptory curtailment of the member states' right to use referendums to deal with the political challenge of integration—is unlikely to pacify constitutional conflicts. Instead, European political elites will have to prove more willing to link popular sovereignty at the national level with EU constitutional reform and be more creative when doing so. Only in this way can EU constitutionalism be more directly linked to the exercise of popular sovereignty.

Notes

1. Altiero Spinelli, "Il modello costituzionale americano e i tentavi di unità europea," in Mario Albertini, ed., *Il Federalismo: Anthologia e definizione* (Bologna: Il Mulino, 1993): 265. My translation.
2. Spinelli, "Il modello costituzionale americano," 267.
3. Spinelli, "Il modello costituzionale americano," 269–70.
4. Spinelli, "Il modello costituzionale americano," 270.
5. Spinelli, "Il modello costituzionale americano," 269.
6. Martha Derthick, *Keeping the Compound Republic: Essays on Federalism* (Washington, D.C.: Brookings Institution, 2001): 45.
7. Spinelli, "Il modello costituzionale americano," 269.
8. Spinelli, "Il modello costituzionale americano," 269.
9. Spinelli, "Il modello costituzionale americano," 270.
10. Samuel Huntington, "Political Modernization: America vs. Europe," *World Politics* 18, no. 3 (April 1966): 378–414, 393.
11. Derthick, *Compound Republic*, 45.
12. Alexander Hamilton et al., *The Federalist* (Cambridge: Cambridge University Press, 2003): 104.
13. See Herbert Storing, *The Anti-Federalist: An Abridgement* (Chicago: University of Chicago Press, 1985).
14. Forrest MacDonald, *States' Rights and the Union: Imperium in Imperio, 1776–1876* (Lawrence: University of Kansas Press, 2000): 43.
15. This line of reasoning was most famously expressed by Chief Justice John Marshall, in *McCulloch v. Maryland* (1819): "from these conventions the Constitution derives its whole authority. The government proceeds directly from the people. . . . The assent of the States in their sovereign capacity is implied in calling a convention, and thus submitting that instrument to the people. But the people were at perfect liberty to accept or reject it; and their act was final. It required not the affirmance, and could not be negatived, by the State governments. The constitution, when thus adopted, was of complete obligation and bound the states." Quoted in Leonard Baker, *John Marshall: A Life in Law* (New York: Macmillan, 1974): 595.

16. Jonathan Elliot, *Elliot's Debates*, 4 (Washington, D.C.: Taylor & Mauray, 1836): 589.

17. Elliot, *Debates*, 589.

18. Lacy K. Ford Jr., "Inventing the Concurrent Majority: Madison, Calhoun, and the Problem of Majoritarianism in American Political Thought," *Journal of Southern History* 60, no. 1 (February 1944): 19–58, 45.

19. Theodore Lowi, "Eurofederalism: What Can European Union Learn from the United States," in Anand Menon and Martin A. Schain, eds., *Comparative Federalism: The European Union and the United States in Comparative Perspective* (Oxford: Oxford University Press, 2006): 93–117.

20. For instance, Case 29/69 *Stauder* [1969] ECR 419, para. 7, Case 11/70 *Internationale Handelsgesellschaft* [1970] ECR 1125, para. 4.

21. Hamilton, *Federalist*, 68.

22. The effectiveness of opting out is by no means guaranteed. For instance, Denmark's Amsterdam opt-out from Title IV provisions (visas, asylum, immigration, and other policies related to free movement of persons) has in practice meant rather little since Denmark's government has obtained "intergovernmental parallel agreements associating Denmark with legislative measures under Title IV." Rebecca Adler-Nissen, "Organized Duplicity? When States Opt Out of the European Union," in Rebecca Adler-Nissen and Thomas Gammeltoft-Hansen (eds.) *Sovereignty Games: Instrumentalizing State Sovereignty in a European and Global Context* (New York: Palgrave, 2008): 81–103, 95. Ironically, the real difference is that by opting out Denmark has no influence on the rules it subsequently signs up to.

23. Hamilton, *Federalist*, 67.

24. Dieter Hanf "Flexibility Clauses in the Founding Treaties, from Rome to Nice," in Bruno de Witte *et al.* (eds.), *The Many Faces of Differentiation in EU Law* (New York: Intersentia, 2001): 3–26, 17.

25. Sergio Fabbrini, "Madison in Brussels: The EU and the U.S. as Compound Democracies," *European Political Science* 4, no. 2 (June 2005): 188–98, 188.

26. John Coultrap, "From Parliamentarism to Pluralism: Models of Democracy and the European Union's 'Democratic Deficit,'" *Journal of Theoretical Politics* 11, no. 1 (1999): 107–35.

27. Erik Oddvar Eriksen and John Erik Fossum, "Democracy through Strong Publics in the European Union?" *Journal of Common Market Studies* 40, no. 3 (September 2002): 401–24.

28. Michael Zürn, "Democratic Governance Beyond the Nation-State: The EU and Other International Institutions," *European Journal of International Relations* 6, no. 2 (June 2000): 183–221.

29. Simon Hix, *What's Wrong with the European Union and How to Fix It* (Oxford: Polity, 2008).

30. This gap is further illustrated by the rise of anti-EU parties and their success in certain member states in EP elections, which suggests that conventional domestic parties have shirked politicizing integration. See Peter Mair, "Political Opposition

and the European Union," *Government and Opposition* 42, no. 1 (September 2009): 1–17.

31. Philippe Schmitter, *How to Democratize the European Union—And Why Bother?* (Lanham: Rowman & Littlefield, 2000).

32. Subsidiarity, the principle supposed to settle competence issues, has proven a stillborn mechanism for deciding the level at which competences are to be exercised.

33. Spinelli, "Il modello costituzionale americano," 270.

34. Theodore Lowi, "Eurofederalism: What Can European Union Learn from the United States."

35. Spinelli, "Il modello costituzionale americano," 269.

36. Bruce Ackerman, *We the People: Foundations* (Cambridge, MA: Belknap, 1991); *We the People: Transformations* (Cambridge, MA: Belknap, 1998).

37. Spinelli, "Il modello costituzionale americano," 268.

38. Giandomenico Majone, *Dilemmas of Integration: The Ambiguities and Pitfalls of Integration by Stealth* (Oxford: Oxford University Press, 2005): 127.

39. Schmitter, *How to Democratize the European Union*, 84–106.

PART THREE

POLITICAL ACTORS AND THE INSTITUTIONAL DIMENSION

CHAPTER FIVE

The Question of Treaty Architecture

From the "Spinelli Draft" to the Lisbon Treaty

Bruno de Witte

The term "Spinelli Draft," mentioned in the title of this contribution, is commonly used as an alternative denomination for what is officially known as the Draft Treaty on European Union, which was adopted by the European Parliament by means of a non–legally binding resolution on 14 February 1984. The European Parliament did not, and does not, have the power to adopt international treaties. The text adopted in its resolution was therefore only a "draft" of a treaty, which did not have any legal effects by itself. The European Parliament had "simply" prepared the ground, and it proposed that the member states of the European Communities should approve, sign and ratify this Draft, thus turning it into a treaty that would transform the EC into a more closely integrated European Union. As is explained further in the text, the Draft was never turned into a Treaty text, and the Treaty on European Union which was enacted by the member states some years later did not resemble the EP's draft of 1984. Whereas Altiero Spinelli was only one among the many MEPs who voted for the adoption of this text, his role was highly important both in initiating this political project and in seeing it to the end despite the many political obstacles on its way and it is therefore politically justified, even if formally inaccurate, to call this text the "Spinelli Draft." I will not directly discuss the course and content of this, Spinelli's last major political battle; it is studied by other contributors to this volume.[1] I will rather examine the "afterlife" of the Spinelli Draft by focusing on one of the Draft's salient characteristics, namely the innovative "Treaty architecture" which it proposed. That innovation, which consisted in integrating the various treaties and organizations of European integration under the new common roof of a "European Union," is now effectively realized, twenty-five-years later, with the entry into force on 1 December 2009 of the Treaty of Lisbon. However, the path leading to this unified structure was very tortuous, and the end result does not quite correspond to the proto-federal institutional system which Spinelli had imagined in the early 1980s.

The term "Treaty architecture" has become a term of art among European Union scholars and politicians. It refers to the way in which the Treaties and annexed Protocols on which the European Union is founded are arranged in relation to each other, and also to the internal structure of those Treaties. It refers, one could say with some exaggeration, to the way the Treaties look before one examines their actual content. This may seem a very technical and politically unimportant matter, but in the European Union, the question of Treaty architecture has become, on several occasions, a matter of constitutional politics. The Spinelli-inspired Draft Treaty on European Union of 1984 was a clear example of the use of Treaty architecture in a context of constitutional reform. Similarly, the Lisbon Treaty is also an attempt to use Treaty architecture in order to make a statement of constitutional politics: in this case, the dismemberment of the Constitutional Treaty, which the Lisbon Treaty effects, was a way for the governments assembled in the IGC to tell their public opinion that the "constitutional moment" was over.

The Question of Treaty Architecture in Spinelli's Time

From the start, the integration process of the "smaller Europe" (as it was then known in contrast with the larger Council of Europe that had been set up in 1950), was marked by the coexistence of several international organizations. In 1957, the Treaty of Rome established the European Economic Community and the European Atomic Energy Community alongside each other and alongside the existing European Coal and Steel Community Treaty, instead of forming a single consolidated organization based on a single treaty. The multiplication of treaties raised concerns primarily because it was accompanied by a duplication of certain institutions: the Commission (the executive body of the EEC and EAEC) was created alongside the High Authority (which had run and continued to run the ECSC), and there were separate Councils of Ministers as well.[2] This was quickly remedied by the *Traité de fusion* of 1965.[3] This "Merger Treaty" (as it was later called in English) created a set of common institutions for the Communities but did not merge these

Communities themselves for fear, probably, that the supranational specificity and interventionist ethos of the ECSC Treaty might be lost.[4] However, the coexistence of three different European Communities was not perceived as a serious problem for the following fifteen years. It was slightly annoying, perhaps, for teaching purposes, and it formed an interesting subject for theoretical reflections on whether or not the Communities formed one single legal order,[5] but it was not a major source of concern in terms of institutional performance or democratic legitimacy. By the early 1980s, however, concern started to grow about the fragmentation between the EC system and the newly developed and institutionally separate European Political Cooperation in foreign affairs (EPC).[6] One of the aims of the Single European Act (an aim expressed by the use of the word "single") was to connect these two institutional strands more closely, but the Act did not effectively achieve that aim. The transformation of EPC into CFSP by the Treaty of Maastricht was a much more important step toward narrowing the gap with the European Community system, but the gap remained. The Treaty of Maastricht marked, indeed, the start of a new and more vigorous debate about treaty architecture due to the creation of a European Union and to the various opt-outs provided for individual countries and groups of countries.

These reforms accomplished by the SEA and the Treaty of Maastricht were essentially member-state driven and their concerns were pragmatic. The states were facing the question of how to use the treaty instrument for creating European institutional structures that would optimally fit the policy developments that had been happening in a piecemeal and uncoordinated way over the years. This has led to "a legal order in which different layers have been successively added, in line with the functional method of achieving what was possible—where the logic of compromise marking intergovernmental agreements took precedence over the need for systematic consistency."[7]

However, there was also a very different approach to Treaty architecture, which was *constitutionally* inspired rather than pragmatic, and in which reforms of treaty structures were intended to pave the way for (rather than follow and codify) a substantive deepening of the integration process. This second strand was represented by the supranational institutions: the Commission first, but above all the Parliament. The Commission had already adopted in 1975 a now entirely forgotten Report on European Union,[8] which was its contribution to the preparation of the now almost forgotten *Tindemans Report*.[9] In its report, the Commission advocated the transformation of the European Communities into a new European Union and the adoption, for that purpose, of an Act of Constitution. This Act would have been given the legal form of an international treaty but would undoubtedly have been constitutional by its aspiration, content, and language. The European Council took hardly any action following these Commission proposals or the Tindemans report itself, apart from approving the general idea of a gradual transformation of the European Communities into a European Union.[10] However, no concrete steps were taken to start this transformation.

A conceptually similar but politically much more incisive challenge to the established treaty regime was made by the first directly elected European Parliament when approving its Draft Treaty establishing the European Union on 14 February 1984.[11] There was a personal connection with the earlier Commission document, because the commissioner responsible for the 1975 document, Altiero Spinelli, was also, in his new capacity of member of the European Parliament, the driving force behind the Draft Treaty. The Parliament's Draft Treaty aimed primarily at a substantive deepening of the integration process and at a major reshuffling of the institutional balance (to the advantage of the European Parliament itself), within an overall perspective of constitutional transformation. In terms of Treaty architecture, the Draft Treaty on European Union prefigured the constitutional reform debates that were to take place in 2000 to 2003.

- It brought together, within a single Treaty text, the Communities and two forms of cooperation that had been developed outside the Community institutional structure, namely European Political Cooperation and the European Monetary System.
- It proposed a reordering of existing institutional rules and principles in a more systematic way. This involved paying greater attention to matters which the EEC Treaty did not deal with (or dealt with in a cursory way) such as the division of powers between the Union and the member states, and the hierarchy of norms of Union law.
- The Draft Treaty itself only contained the fundamental institutional provisions, while the more detailed provisions of primary law would—according to the Draft—continue to be found, at first, in the Community Treaties and, later on, in "organic laws" to be adopted (and revised) by the institutions of the Union. These new laws would gradually, as they were being adopted, replace the old Community treaty text. The Treaty would therefore only contain the core rules of the EU's institutional and substantive regime.

Thus, for the European Parliament, the proposed reorganization of the treaties was inspired by a broader objective of global constitutional reform.

The existing three Communities would gradually disappear and be replaced by a more integrated organization, the European Union. As we saw, the member state governments, when negotiating the Single European Act shortly afterward, declined to follow the roadmap proposed by the Parliament, but instead decided to keep the European Communities in existence. They simply tied European Political Cooperation a bit more closely to the Communities but without fully integrating it into a common legal structure. The move to create a European Union happened only five years later, at the Maastricht summit of December 1991, and its significance was contrary to the European Parliament's aspirations when it adopted its Draft Treaty on European Union; the newly created European Union diluted the existing Community law framework rather than upgrading it.

The Question of Treaty Architecture in and after Maastricht: The Coexistence of the European Community and the European Union

The Maastricht Treaty created, alongside the existing three European Communities, a new "entity"[12] called the European Union. This more complex Treaty architecture became known almost immediately as the "pillar structure," although that term was not used in the official documents at the time of Maastricht.[13] The European Union's delayed creation (when seen from the vantage point of the Spinelli Draft) embodied a legal and political paradox, in the following sense: whereas the notion of "European Union" had been frequently used in pre-Maastricht times (and particularly in Spinelli's thinking) to indicate possible new arrangements for a *more integrated* Europe, the real-life European Union established in Maastricht was seen by many, and not without good reasons, as a *step back* in the European integration process, since that name was used to cover two new forms of interstate cooperation, in common foreign and security policy (CFSP) and justice and home affairs (JHA), which were marked by a lesser degree of supranationalism than the existing European Community—so, not a leap forward toward a federal Europe, but a return to more traditional forms of intergovernmental cooperation, even though the reach of the EU's policies was extended compared to the pre-Maastricht regime.

The idea of creating the European Union as a new and separate organization arose almost fortuitously in the course of the Intergovernmental Conference leading up to the Maastricht Treaty. In fact, the Dutch Presidency had, in September 1991, presented a draft treaty text that included the new policy fields of common foreign and security policy, and justice and home affairs, within the existing institutional framework of the European Community.[14] One of the main reasons for the rejection of that draft was the view of a number of national governments that the Community legal framework would unduly constrain the intergovernmental mode of decision making which they preferred to use in these two new fields of cooperation. In the end, a hybrid institutional structure was adopted which included the new policy domains within the encompassing framework of a newly created European Union, thus keeping them *outside* the existing European Community framework. However, one could easily have achieved this same objective, namely of shielding Common Foreign and Security Policy and Justice and Home Affairs from the "pernicious" supranational features of the Community method, without the cumbersome and confusing pillar construction. Close observers of the Maastricht negotiations have confirmed that, technically speaking, one could have done one of two things: either integrate the new forms of cooperation within the framework of the EC Treaty whilst making exceptions and derogations to the Treaty's normal rules, or (the route which was eventually taken at Maastricht) establish forms of cooperation under a new treaty linked to the existing treaties by means of so-called common provisions.[15]

The road taken in the autumn of 1991 had long-term implications for the structural evolution of European law. By establishing the European Union, the Maastricht Treaty marked the beginning of the end of the European Community; imperceptibly, it started a process which has led, today, to the complete absorption of the European Community by the European Union.

Whereas the political reasons for the adoption of the pillar structure at Maastricht are clear, it proved to be difficult to make logical sense of the rather baroque Treaty architecture that was put in place by the Maastricht Treaty. The academic debate on this new architecture evolved imperceptibly during the 1990s.[16] At first, the dominant view, taken especially by Community law scholars, was one of unconcealed dislike of the new construction. Some of them considered that the European Union, which had been proudly "established" by Article 1 of the EU Treaty, did not have any formal legal existence of its own. The Union was viewed by them as little more than a framework located outside the EC within which the institutions of the European Community acted in conjunction with the Member States—a metaphorical place rather than an actual organization. However, another, and simpler, account rapidly gained ground among the institutional experts. It emphasized the fact that, as Article 3 EU Treaty affirmed, there was a single institutional framework with common institutions *of the European Union* acting within the context of the various pillars, albeit under specific rules for each of the pillars. Among the political actors, the latter view became quickly dominant, as it corresponded to the way they experienced their daily activities in Brussels, Luxembourg or Strasbourg. The overarching and encompassing nature of the European Union—as compared to the European Community—was spelled out, in a tone of insouciant self-evidence, at the start of the Laeken Declaration adopted by the European Council in December 2001: "The European Union currently has four Treaties. The objectives, powers and policy instruments of the Union are currently spread across those Treaties."

Following this approach, the European Union could, indeed, best be considered as a "layered organization" within which the European Community, the European Atomic Energy Community, and (until its demise in 2002) the European Coal and Steel Community operated as autonomous sub-organizations with their own legal personality (including the capacity to conclude international agreements with third countries).[17]

The evolution of the architecture debate after Maastricht was marked by two further elements. First, there was the gradual acknowledgement that the European Union, far from being a transitional "stop-gap" construction, was a stable legal reality with a lasting role in the European integration process. Secondly, there was a growing understanding that the European Union was not a radically different thing from the European Community, and that both organizations had many legal principles and organizational practices in common.

This evolution had implications for the way in which a future merger of the Treaties was viewed. At first, the main goal of those advocating a merger was to bring the intergovernmental pillars back in "from the cold," into the safe haven of the European Community, whereas the idea of a merger was resisted by those in the intergovernmental camp who feared that the distinctive institutional characteristics of the second and third pillars would thereby be lost. Later on, toward the end of the 1990s, the prospect of a merger of the Treaties became gradually less controversial: on the one hand, the *communautaristes* had little hope that the intergovernmental features of the second and third pillars could be wiped out entirely, whereas, on the other hand, the intergovernmental-minded did not dispute the fact that all three pillars were part of a single institutional framework and subject to a set of common legal principles, and they became aware of the practical complications caused by the separation of the Treaties.

However, the first post-Maastricht Intergovernmental Conference, the one leading to the Treaty of Amsterdam, came too early for the idea of the merger of the Treaties to have gathered enough support. In 1995 and 1996, the European Parliament had sponsored several research projects on the way in which the various European Treaties could be amalgamated into one text. One project was elaborated by Professor Bieber[18]; another one was prepared by the European University Institute and was entitled: *Unified and Simplified Model of the European Community Treaties and the Treaty on European Union in Just One Treaty*.[19] However, the member state governments were distinctly cooler toward this idea than the Parliament. Admittedly, the European Council meeting in Florence in June 1996 had called on the post-Maastricht IGC (which had just started then) "to seek all possible ways of simplifying the Treaties so as to make the Union's goals and operation easier for the public to understand."[20] This aim was formally reflected, one year later, in the short Part Two of the Amsterdam Treaty which was entitled *Simplification*. However, on a closer look, these provisions simplified very little: they essentially repealed some lapsed and obsolete provisions of the EC, ECSC, and EAEC Treaties, and they also rephrased, but only to a very limited extent, some of the remaining provisions.[21] In addition to this, the Amsterdam Treaty contained, in its Final Act, "consolidated" (i.e., updated) versions of both the EC Treaty and the EU Treaty. These consolidated and renumbered texts became *de facto* the reference used by all practitioners, and indeed by the European Courts, notwithstanding the fact that, formally speaking, they had no binding legal value since they were included in the Final Act only "for illustrative purposes." A further operation of token simplification happened in the aftermath of Amsterdam. On the basis of a mandate given to it by the Amsterdam summit, the General Secretariat of the Council prepared and released a draft *single* treaty, merging the existing Treaties without modifying the text of their individual provisions. However, this was done, again, "for illustrative purposes" only—to show what a future "single Treaty" could possibly look like—and it did not attract much political or legal attention at the time.

When all was said and done, the Treaty of Amsterdam had left in existence two separate Treaties, the EC Treaty and EU Treaty, and had confirmed the existence of three separate pillars. Whereas some national governments had insisted on including, in the Maastricht Treaty, a rendezvous clause providing for a Treaty revision in 1996 in order to be able to abolish the pillar structure as soon as possible, when that Treaty revision took place (at Amsterdam) the pillar structure proved sufficiently resilient still: what seemed a rather scandalous anomaly in the steady progress of European integration for countries like the Netherlands and Belgium, and for many observers, back in 1991, had become an accepted feature of the *fin-de-siècle* European Union.

At the same time, the Treaty of Amsterdam showed the robustness and power of attraction of the first pillar. The robustness of the Community model was shown by the fact that the role of all three supranational institutions, European Parliament, Commission, and Court of Justice, was confirmed or reinforced. Given the fact that the Treaty revision process was still solidly in the hands of the member states, the explanation for the resilience of the Community model must be that the national governments themselves had come to recognize—some more willingly than others—that they had been too clever by half in the Autumn of 1991 when they broke the European Community mould and invented unprecedented procedures and entirely new legal instruments. The procedures of the second and third pillars had proved to be cumbersome and inefficient, and the new legal instruments, particularly those chosen for the third pillar, had proved to be blunt and legally ambiguous. It was out of a better understanding of their own long-term national interest that the Member States decided, in Amsterdam, to "inject" the two intergovernmental pillars with an extra dose of *méthode communautaire*, but without abolishing them altogether.

The Recent Treaty Reform (2002 to 2009): Absorption of the European Community by the European Union

The Nice Treaty, which was agreed in December 2000, and which contained a further piecemeal revision of the EC and EU Treaties, was generally a very low key affair and the question of Treaty architecture was not even broached during the negotiations. However, on the fringes of the Nice IGC, the European Commission had asked the European University Institute in Florence to produce a feasibility study on a new idea (though echoing a theme of the Spinelli Draft): whether it would be possible to integrate the various treaties in a single text whilst distinguishing, within that integrated text, between the fundamental and less fundamental norms, so as to produce greater clarity about the main institutional and substantive norms governing the European Union. The EUI study on the "reorganization" of the Treaties, which was presented in May 2000, showed how this could be done on the basis of the existing texts of the EC Treaty and EU Treaty.[22] The favorable political response to this report, on the part of the European Commission, the European Parliament, and some of the member states, eventually led to the inclusion of the treaty simplification theme in the Declaration on the

Future of the Union, adopted by the Nice summit in December 2000, as one of four reform themes on which the governments agreed to start a "wider and deeper debate," but the Declaration did not specify what precisely was meant by the term "simplification" which, as we saw, had been given a distinctly unambitious meaning in the context of the Amsterdam Treaty some years before.

The European Council's Laeken Declaration, adopted one year later (in December 2001), spelled out the enigmatic reference of the Nice Declaration, and confirmed that a reorganization of the Treaty architecture would be an important item on the reform agenda, although that agenda was being broadened, at the same time, by the inclusion of a host of other reform issues, which were listed in the form of questions. It may be helpful, for the purpose of this paper, to cite the relevant paragraphs of the Declaration in full:

Toward a Constitution for European Citizens

> The European Union currently has four Treaties. The objectives, powers and policy instruments of the Union are currently spread across those Treaties. If we are to have greater transparency, simplification is essential.
>
> Four sets of questions arise in this connection. The first concerns simplifying the existing Treaties without changing their content. Should the distinction between the Union and the Communities be reviewed? What of the division into three pillars?
>
> Questions then arise as to the possible reorganization of the Treaties. Should a distinction be made between a basic treaty and the other treaty provisions? Should this distinction involve separating the texts? Could this lead to a distinction between the amendment and ratification procedures for the basic treaty and for the other treaty provisions?
>
> Thought would also have to be given to whether the Charter of Fundamental Rights should be included in the basic treaty and to whether the European Community should accede to the European Convention on Human Rights.
>
> The question ultimately arises as to whether this simplification and reorganization might not lead in the long run to the adoption of a constitutional text in the Union. What might the basic features of such a constitution be? The values which the Union cherishes, the fundamental rights and obligations of its citizens, the relationship between Member States in the Union?

One may note that the European Council, in its Laeken Declaration, elaborated the little phrase contained in the Nice Declaration one year earlier by operating a distinction between what it called "simplification" and "reorganization." *Simplification* was defined as a reconsideration of the need to keep the EC and EU treaties separate, which was a broader aim than what was covered by the same term in the Amsterdam Treaty. *Reorganization* (in French: *réaménagement*) referred to the identification of a basic content within the treaties and its separation from other, non-basic treaty provisions.[23] Both these ideas were indeed taken on board by the Convention on the Future of the Union which started its constitution-drafting work soon after.

On the question of the merger of the EC Treaty and EU Treaty into one common text,[24] a consensus was reached fairly early in the Convention's life, in the framework of the working group on Legal Personality which was ably steered by its chairman Giuliano Amato toward the conclusion that a full-scale merger of the two separate organizations (the EC and the EU) was needed and therefore also of the two treaties on which those organizations were based. This conclusion, in turn, paved the way for the reorganization into four separate Parts of the common Treaty. The decisive moment for the adoption of this revolutionary approach to treaty architecture was October 2002, when the Presidium of the Convention presented its "Draft European Constitution" (since it only indicated the main lines but did not present a full text—unlike the EP's Draft Treaty of 1984—it was called, somewhat disrespectfully, "the skeleton").[25] After that moment, and given the favorable reception of the skeleton, the basic choice in favor of a Treaty merger and reorganization was no longer called into question and survived until the signature by the member state governments of the Constitutional Treaty, in October 2004.

The decision to merge the European Community and the European Union inevitably involved a choice about the denomination of the newly unified organization. To some, the hallowed name "Community" may have sounded more appealing, but it was very quickly decided that the new organization would instead be called "European Union." As mentioned above, the member state governments, and the European institutions themselves, had by then adopted the habit of speaking about the European Union in generic terms even when they referred to policies or measures that were formally being adopted in the framework of the Community. The merger was formally laid down in two provisions of the Constitutional Treaty. Article IV-437, one of its final provisions, was entitled "Repeal of earlier Treaties" and stated that "[t]his Treaty establishing a Constitution for Europe shall repeal the Treaty establishing the European Community, the Treaty on European Union," as well as all the accession and revision treaties that had supplemented the EC Treaty and the EU Treaty. In order to fill the void created by this repeal, Article I-1 stated that "this Constitution establishes the European Union" as the new overarching organization replacing the European Community and the "old" European Union.

In this manner, the "bits and pieces" which the Maastricht Treaty had left in its wake[26] were reassembled into an overall structure. The merger operation was a very welcome reform, and one that did not provoke any opposition on the part of individual governments during the IGC that adopted the Constitutional Treaty. Nor was it controversial during the subsequent French and Dutch referendum campaigns. However, it became a collateral victim of the ratification crisis that occurred in 2005 after those referendums.

When the Brussels European Council of June 2007, after a two-year-long *pause de réflexion*, decided to bury the Constitutional Treaty, it also decided to undo the repeal of the existing Treaties, and instead to use those two Treaties as the recipients within which most of the substantive reforms contained in the Constitutional Treaty would be reinserted. To put it in the words used in the European Council's Conclusions: "The constitutional concept, which consisted in repealing all existing Treaties and replacing them by a single text called 'Constitution' is abandoned. The Reform Treaty will introduce into the existing Treaties, which remain in force, the innovations resulting from the 2004 IGC."

So, the content of the Constitutional Treaty was split into two parts, with one part to be incorporated in the EU Treaty and a much bigger part in the EC Treaty. A third segment of the Constitutional Treaty, namely its Part II containing the Charter of Rights, was to be hidden from sight outside the two Treaties, and to lead a separate existence as an instrument having the same legal status as the two Treaties, which effectively meant that it became a third basic Treaty, alongside the two others, thereby complicating even further the new post-constitutional treaty architecture.

However, the merger of the European Community and the European Union into one single organization was one of the achievements of the constitutional heydays of 2002 to 2003 which seemed too valuable to abandon, and the European Council, at its meeting of June 2007, chose to preserve it for the future. This merger implied, obviously, that the EC Treaty could no longer keep its existing name, since the "Community" would no longer exist. This is why the revised EC Treaty was given the inelegant new name of "Treaty on the Functioning of the European Union."

Now that the Lisbon Treaty—as devised by the European Council in June 2007—has entered into force, on 1 December 2009, the architectural story will provisionally end with a paradox. Whereas the Treaty architecture inaugurated by the Treaty of Maastricht consisted of two separate treaties corresponding to two separate but interconnected organizations (the EC and the EU), and whereas the Constitutional Treaty had proposed a radical simplification by moving to one single organization and one single treaty, the

Lisbon Treaty leaves in existence two separate treaties (the EU Treaty and the Treaty on the Functioning of the EU), but only one single organization which is established and regulated by those treaties, namely the European Union. There is, in fact, no logical explanation for the decision to keep two separate treaties, the only explanation being of a tactical-political nature: to make it appear that the Constitutional Treaty is effectively dead and buried, it seemed advisable to the national governments to artificially keep in place the existing treaties, even though one of the amendments to the "existing" EC Treaty will be to modify its name and thereby to end the long and successful life of the European Community. The European Union, on the other hand, will continue its strange career: it originally embodied the political dreams and preferences of the European federalists such as Spinelli; then it became an obscure legal object at Maastricht, after which it was gradually acknowledged to be the overarching organization of the European integration process, and now it has entirely absorbed the European Community—but without realizing at all Altiero Spinelli's vision of the 1970s and 1980s of a European Union that would have symbolized, by its creation, a step toward a more closely integrated Europe, and would have pushed that integration process further toward a federal end-goal.

Notes

1. See also the literature cited in note 11.

2. On the contrary, a single Parliament and a single Court of Justice were set up right from the beginning, through the *Convention on certain institutions common to the European Communities*, which entered into force at the same time as the EEC and EAEC Treaties.

3. See, for a contemporary account of this operation, Jean-Victor Louis, "La fusion des institutions des Communautés européennes," *Revue du marché commun* 97 (1966): 843–56.

4. Ulrich Everling, "From European Communities to European Union—by Convergence to Consistency," in Armin von Bogdandy, Paul Mavroidis and Yves Mény (eds.), *European Integration and International Co-ordination. Studies in Transnational Law in Honour of Claus-Dieter Ehlermann* (The Hague: Kluwer Law International, 2002): 139–58, 141.

5. On this question, see e.g., the study by Albert Bleckmann, "Die Einheit der Europäischen Gemeinschaftsrechtsordnung. Einheit oder Mehrheit der Europäischen Gemeinschaften," *Europarecht* 13 (1978): 95–104.

6. The amalgamation of the Community and EPC structures was one of the central aims of the so-called Genscher/Colombo proposals made jointly by the German and Italian governments in November 1981; see Pauline Neville-Jones, "The

Genscher/Colombo proposals on European Union," *Common Market Law Review* 20, no.4 (1983): 657–700. On the institutional practice in those years, see S. Nuttall, "Interaction between European Political Cooperation and the European Community," *Yearbook of European Law* 7 (1987): 211–50.

7. G. L. Tosato, "Simplification of the Treaties as a Constitutional Process," in *Institutional Reforms in the European Union—Memorandum for the Convention* (Rome: EuropEos, 2002): 185.

8. Report on European Union of 26 June 1975, *Bulletin of the European Communities*, Suppl. 5/75.

9. *European Union—Report by Mr Leo Tindemans, Prime Minister of Belgium, to the European Council*, in *Bulletin of the European Communities*, Suppl. 1/1976. On the content and context of the Tindemans Report, see Michael Burgess, *Federalism and European Union: The Building of Europe, 1950–2000* (London: Routledge, 2000): 106–16.

10. European Council of The Hague, November 1976, *Bulletin of the European Communities* 11 (1976): 93–94.

11. *Official Journal of the European Communities* 1984, C 77/33. For the political history of the Draft Treaty, see Richard Corbett, *The European Parliament's Role in Closer EU Integration* (Basingstoke: Palgrave, 1998): chapters 6 and 7. For a legal commentary, see Francesco Capotorti et al., *The European Union Treaty: Commentary on the Draft Adopted by the EP on 14 February 1984* (Oxford: Oxford University Press, 1986). For a reflection on the Draft Treaty (and later constitutional initiatives of the EP) in the context of the current constitutional reform debate, see Jean-Victor Louis, "Les projets de constitution dans l'histoire de la construction européenne," in Paul Magnette (ed.), *La constitution de l'Europe* (Brussels: Editions de l'Université de Bruxelles, 2000) and, more recently, Jean-Victor Louis, "Du projet Spinelli à la Constitution européenne," in Christine Kaddous and Andreas Auer (eds.), *Les principes fondamentaux de la Constitution européenne* (Basle: Helbing & Lichtenhahn, 2006).

12. I deliberately use this vague term "entity" in order not to prejudge the question of the legal qualification of the European Union, to which I return later on in this chapter.

13. The term "pillars" was acknowledged by the European Council some years later; see Conclusions of the Dublin European Council, December 1996.

14. Finn Laursen and Sophie Vanhoonacker, *The Intergovernmental Conference on Political Union* (Maastricht: European Institute of Public Administration, 1992). The Dutch draft was published in *Agence Europe Documents*, No. 1733/1734 of 3 October 1991.

15. J. Cloos, G. Reinesch, D. Vignes and J. Weyland, *Le Traité de Maastricht. Genèse, analyse, commentaires*. (Brussels: Bruylant, 1993).

16. For a synthetic account of this academic debate, with further references, see Deirdre Curtin, "Emerging institutional parameters and organised difference in the European Union," in Bruno de Witte, Dominik Hanf and Ellen Vos (eds.), *The Many Faces of Differentiation in EU Law* (Antwerp: Intersentia, 2001): 351–54.

17. See, for a fuller exposition of this view, Bruno de Witte, "The Pillar Structure and the Nature of the European Union: Greek Temple or French Gothic Cathedral?" in T. Heukels, N. Blokker, M. Brus (eds.), *The European Union after Amsterdam* (The Hague: Kluwer Law International, 1998); and Deirdre Curtin and Ige Dekker, "The EU as a 'Layered' International Organization: Institutional Unity in Disguise," in Paul Craig and Gráinne de Búrca (eds.), *The Evolution of EU Law* (Oxford: Oxford University Press, 1999).

18. *Un projet de traité consolidé de l'Union européenne*, Parlement européen, Série politique W-17, December 1995.

19. See a short presentation of this study by Armin von Bogdandy and Claus-Dieter Ehlermann, "Consolidation of European Treaties: Feasibility, Costs and Benefits," *Common Market Law Review*, 33, no. 6 (1996): 1107–9.

20. Conclusions of the European Council in Florence, 21–22 June 1996, *Bulletin of the European Union* 6, no. 1 (1996): 7.

21. For a detailed official commentary of this operation, see Explanatory Report from the General Secretariat of the Council on the Simplification of the Community Treaties, OJ 1997, C 353/1. For a semi-official presentation by one of its authors, see Jean-Paul Jacqué, "La simplification et la consolidation des traités," *Revue trimestrielle de droit européen* (1997): 195. See also Christoph U. Schmid, *Ways out of the maquis communautaire: on simplification and consolidation and the need for a restatement of European primary law*, EUI Working Paper RSC no.99/6.

22. Robert Schuman Centre for Advanced Studies (European University Institute, Florence), *A Basic Treaty for the European Union. A Study of the Reorganization of the Treaties* (study coordinated by Yves.Mény and Claus-Dieter Ehlermann), May 2000 (available on http://europa.eu.int/comm/archives/igc2000/offdoc/discussiondocs).

23. This terminological distinction in the Laeken Declaration, between simplification and reorganisation, may not have been made deliberately and was not set in stone. In fact, the term "simplification" was also often used, in the following years, to refer to the broader "reorganisation" operation.

24. The Euratom Treaty was left out of the merger but this had little practical importance.

25. CONV 369/02 of 28 October 2002. On the background of the Presidium's proposal for unification of the treaties, see H. Bribosia, "De la simplification des traités au traité constitutionnel," in Giuliano Amato, Hervé Bribosia and Bruno de Witte (eds.), *Genèse et destinée de la Constitution européenne* (Brussels: Bruylant, 2007): 195–202. On the crucial role of the "skeleton" in the Convention process, see Peter Norman, *The Accidental Constitution: The Story of the European Convention* (Brussels: EuroComment, 2003): 71–76.

26. I borrow from the title of Deirdre Curtin's commentary on the Maastricht Treaty: "The Constitutional Structure of the Union: A Europe of Bits and Pieces," *Common Market Law Review* 30, no. 1 (1993): 17–70.

CHAPTER SIX

François Mitterrand and the Spinelli Treaty of 1984

Support or Instrumentalization?

Jean-Marie Palayret

The second half of the 1980s was arguably the most active and dynamic period in the European integration process since the early 1960s. The traditional interpretation centers on the appointment of Jacques Delors as Commission President in January 1985, in which role his key contribution was to identify a new target for the Community process, implementing the so-called single market program. But to what extent was Spinelli's project also a catalyst for this *relance*? This chapter will try to demonstrate that Spinelli was, three decades after his initiative for creating a European Political Community (EPC) in the early 1950s, once again at the centre of a major endeavor to federate Europe. This time, the Monnet method of building a unified Europe by a series of steps had provided him with a directly elected European Parliament to act as a constituent body. However, to succeed, he needed the full support of France, which held the European Economic Community presidency in the first half of 1984. Despite a very encouraging statement of intentions by François Mitterrand in Strasbourg in May 1984, the result—the European Single Act (1986)—did not meet Spinelli's expectations.

The European Parliament: The Driving Force of the Project

Spinelli had actually been in Brussels from 1972 as one of Italy's two commissioners and had served there with some distinction, but it was after 1979 with the first election of the Strasbourg Assembly by direct universal suffrage that he really came out of the shadows, at the age of seventy-two, standing for the European Parliament. He chose to sit as an independent Member of the European Parliament (MEP) affiliated to the communist group.[1]

Spinelli first showed his hand on 25 June 1980, when the European Parliament refused to adopt the Council's draft Community budget in its entirety and thereby plunged Europe into a political and, potentially, a financial crisis.[2] In so doing, Spinelli intended to use the admittedly very limited power Parliament had in the Community decision-making process, and steer through a leveling-off of Common Agricultural Policy spending, while increasing funding for other policies, particularly the structural funds in the less advantaged regions.[3]

On 11 November 1979 Spinelli invited the European Parliament to formulate "precise and concrete proposals" in view of a wide-ranging reform of the European Economic Community's political institutions and became *rapporteur* for a resolution on a Treaty establishing a European Union.[4] In this way, Spinelli tried to convince his fellow MEPs that they must now take the destiny of the European Economic Community into their own hands: "I do not address the Council of Ministers," he told them, "because it has demonstrated its total impotence."[5] He was convinced that the only way to bring a federal union to fruition was for the European Parliament to seize the initiative and to work for total reform of the Treaty of Rome (1957). He argued the view that within a few years the European Economic Community would be enlarged by the addition of three new members (Greece, Spain and Portugal), a prospect which spurred institutional reform.

His first formal step toward this goal came in July 1980 when, with his parliamentary assistant Pier-Virgilio Dastoli, he wrote to his fellows MEPs, inviting their support for a concerted move to further integration. Eight "eager members" responded to his call, meeting at the prestigious Crocodile restaurant in Strasbourg. These included two German (Lucker and Von Wogau) and one Italian (Gaiotti) Christian Democrat, an Italian Communist (Leonardi) and an Italian Republican, (Visentini), two British Labour MEPs, (Balfe and Key) and a lone British Conservative (Stanley Johnson). Membership grew, regular weekly meetings were held and by the end of the year some eighty MEPs had expressed interest. Thus was born the Crocodile Club, a cross-party group open to all MEPs convinced "of the need for European Political Reform of great breadth."[6]

Spinelli aimed to outflank the existing party groupings, which he feared would block the initiative. As he explained in a letter to a colleague:

> The European Parliament is elected using party electoral machines geared to national elections, which do not have European political programmes but a vague trans-national background. . . . Their members are divided substantially into three groups: innovators, eager to advance the Union, immobilists, eager to keep it where it was and to even make it regress, the *marais* ("the swamp"), composed of those who do not know what they want: the innovators are conscious that they must rally around a common policy and, by ignoring party loyalties, they would overcome the prevailing influence of the swamp.[7]

The Crocodile Club was to be the catalyst for "awakening the innovators." The established forum for promoting new ideas was the Political Affairs Committee. But it was dominated by the centre–right European Peoples' Party, hostile to the Communists. Spinelli predicted that the committee would merely give his project a "first-class burial." Instead, he planned an "ad hoc constitutional working group" which he could control. For this he needed a parliamentary resolution, to prepare the ground for which, in October 1980, he launched a periodical "The Crocodile." As expected, his resolution was treated with disdain by the established party groups. The largest group, the Christian Democrats, constituted the main obstacle to any vote on Spinelli's resolution: having been prominent in the European Parliament's integrationist initiatives, they saw Spinelli as an interloper. Even the Communists were reluctant to back him and did so only when Spinelli made a direct appeal to Italy's national Communist leader, Enrico Berlinguer.[8] The Club gradually enlisted support from Socialist MEPs and attracted heavyweight support from the Italian Prime Minister Bettino Craxi and several other leading Social Democrats, including Willy Brandt, Katherina Focke and Erwin Lange (president of the powerful Parliamentary Budget Committee).[9] They were joined, in backing the resolution, by the Liberal Group, under its German leader Martin Bangemann. By this means, the Christian Democrats were isolated.

On 9 July 1981, the Parliament approved the resolution[10] and the Committee on Institutional Affairs, entrusted with the task of working out a modification of the existing treaties, started work in January 1982. Spinelli thus won approval for the European Parliament to assume the initiative fully to give new momentum to the establishment of the European Union. The ad hoc Committee, with Spinelli as its co-coordinator and Mauro Ferri as its President, proved to be very active: to maximize support, it held hearings for a wide range of politicians, trade unions leaders, and academics to give their views. The European Movement and the European Federalist Union were recruited to whip up public support. The Committee's tasks could not have been more ambitious: working with six co-rapporteurs from the different party groups, drafting chapters on the several aspects, its aim was not simply to amend the existing European treaties but to produce an entirely new one.[11]

Mitterrand and the Draft Treaty for European Union: Support or Instrumentalization?

During the second half of 1983, Spinelli and his team worked on what was now officially called a "draft Treaty establishing a European Union." As Paolo Ponzano develops further this theme in his contribution, my own will focus primarily on the role of the French Presidency in the instrumentalization of Spinelli's proposals, under François Mitterrand. The European Parliament adopted the draft by a large majority (by 237 votes for and 31 against with 43 abstentions) in its Resolution of 14 February 1984. It was addressed directly to the governments and parliaments of the member states, to prevent the Council from blocking it. Despite the support of the Strasbourg Assembly and of the Italian government, Spinelli was aware that any change would only be possible within the framework of the intergovernmental process and that his treaty stood little chance of being ratified without heavyweight support. He therefore sought Mitterrand's aid. In his speech in the debate on the adoption of the draft treaty, he exhorted France, which then held the presidency of the Council, to take the initiative in winning support for it among other member states and two months later, on 16 April 1984, he handed a personal note to that effect to the French President during a short audience in Paris, telling him that he hoped the presidency would contribute to the advancement of the project, obliging all the member states "to accept their responsibilities." In particular, he recommended that such an initiative should be taken "apart from the Council of Ministers, to circumvent the role of unanimity."[12] Mitterrand gave his answer on 24 May. In a very high profile speech in Strasbourg he declared he was in favor of the European Parliament's proposals. A new situation demanded a new treaty, which obviously could not replace the existing treaties but could extend them to the domains which were beyond them, and France was available for such an enterprise. It was willing "to examine and defend" Spinelli's project, "the inspiration behind which it approves," and suggested "preparatory discussions" which could lead to a conference of "interested member states."[13]

Mitterrand gave his backing because he greatly needed a European success. Having examined the project for the first time in February, he told his Minister for European Affairs, Roland Dumas: "All of this seems very interesting, that's good. There are some good ideas: we must obviously correct certain points, but we can take up some of the suggestions."[14] France was nearing the end of its presidency of the EEC, and with her economy in recession, her fast-rising unemployment, widespread demonstrations in favor of the *école libre* and his party's failure in the European parliamentary elections, the French President needed a dramatic gesture before his term of office ended.[15] Second, the European Economic Community's institutional system seemed especially in disarray. European Council meetings came to be dominated by ill-tempered exchanges about the Community budget and the British rebate, food surpluses generated by the Common Agricultural Policy or the complex and lengthy talks to admit Spain and Portugal into the European Economic Community. In the spring of 1984, Mitterrand conducted a marathon tour of eight European capitals and judged there was strong support for a new European initiative: as he told the Irish Prime Minister, Garret Fitzgerald, the moment has come "to leave the humdrum routine of technical questions" and to give "the political impetus which could solve Europe's crisis."

However, Mitterrand's support for the Spinelli Project was by no means unconditional. His own Foreign Ministry was strongly opposed to any strengthening of the Community's institutions. To Claude Cheysson, supporting the Spinelli Project would mean "opening Pandora's box."[16] The legal department of the Quai d'Orsay was very anxious about the difficulties the implementation of two distinct juridical systems (European Communities vs. European Union) could raise. The economic department (Guy Legras, Jacques Andreani) therefore suggested that the President had two options in responding to the Treaty. One would be to split it into two parts: its economic proposals (prepared in the Constitutional Committee by the European Parliament's sub-committee chaired by Jacques Moreau) to be put forward as a first step, and discussion of its more ambitious components could then be deferred for five years, when it was intended to reexamine the Solemn Declaration of Stuttgart. The second option would be for France to advance her own counter-proposals.[17] In the event, Mitterrand came up with a combination of the two options, starting with an invitation to heads of state and government to take part in an "informal meeting" in Paris in the autumn, to discuss "political and institutional questions," the application of the Treaty of Rome and any other proposal which might be put forward.[18] The real significance of the advice given to Mitterrand would only become apparent later: it was this which first sowed the idea that the next step forward in the integration of Europe should be in two stages, beginning with a major economic reform, then continuing with a more ambitious "institutional reform."

Herein lay the genesis of the two treaties which would become the Single European Act, ratified in 1986, and the Treaty on European Union, agreed at Maastricht five years later.[19] From a tactical point of view one feature of Spinelli's project which particularly appealed to Mitterrand lay in its radicalism: the diplomatic cell of the Elysée (Pierre Morel, Jean-Louis Bianco, Elisabeth Guigou) in a memo dated 23 August 1984 stated that "To take this document (*sc.* the Spinelli Project) as a basis will mean, from the beginning of the negotiations, to make the distinction between countries which are willing to move ahead (the Founding Six) and the countries which are hesitating or resisting (the other Four)."[20] From a strategic point of view, another key point was the idea of a "two-speed Europe," namely the fact that the Treaty could not be blocked by the veto of any country, such as Britain, which might be reluctant to move on to much fuller integration. In this perspective, the Spinelli draft Treaty presented a crucial advantage: its article 82 stipulated that the Treaty could enter into effect when ratified by over half the member states representing at least two-thirds of the future Union's population.[21] According to the most optimistic, it would be impossible for the reticent states to remain outside the new structure which would replace the Community. The others reckoned that a crisis would be inevitable, considering how impossible it would be to convince Great Britain, Greece, and Denmark to further European integration. Mitterrand confirmed this by his actions at the European Council under French Presidency in Fontainebleau (25–26 June 1984), where he succeeded in setting up a committee of experts (known as the Dooge Committee, after the Irish Senator who chaired it, or "Spaak II" Committee) to consider future institutional reform of the Community and to improve further European cooperation.[22] Each of the heads of governments would have their own personal representative. Mitterrand had in fact already allowed for the possibility that Margaret Thatcher might veto the setting-up of the Dooge Committee, in which case he had planned—with Kohl's agreement—to call openly for a new Messina Conference primarily open to the Six Founding Countries and those countries willing to participate.[23]

At Fontainebleau, the European Economic Community had fortunately cleared most of the technical issues which dominated its agenda, the conflict over the budget and the thorny issue of Spanish-Portuguese enlargement. The Community would now be free to launch the new stage of institutional reform. For Mitterrand this had become an absolute necessity: "With twelve members, the Community integrates heterogeneous interests, contrary traditions, rival ambitions. The present Community is more fragile than that of yesterday, and there is no longer just one cure for all its ills: for a larger Community, stronger institutions are needed."[24] Mitterrand ensured that he kept a guiding hand on the Committee's work, by nominating as his representative Maurice Faure, a "convinced European" who became its "spokesman," responsible for orchestrating its activities. Moreover, the Committee was externally controlled by Mitterrand's and Kohl's close advisers, the "sherpas" Jacques Attali and Horst Teltschick.[25] Their objective was focused on the construction of a political Europe through intergovernmental cooperation, directed by a Secretariat. The majority of the Dooge Committee, in any case, recognized the value of Spinelli's project. They were in favor of a "true political entity" and wanted an intergovernmental conference (IGC) to prepare a treaty of European union. This IGC should take as its starting point "the spirit and the method of the project voted by the European Parliament."[26] But the interim report that the Dooge Committee presented at the Dublin European Council, favoring an "intergovernmental Conference to prepare a new Treaty," was immediately contested by the United Kingdom, Denmark, and Greece, opposing institutional reform and any need for such a Treaty. When the final report was presented to the Brussels Council, no decision was taken. Margaret Thatcher at this time was focused on a wholly different initiative: her chief contribution to the Brussels Council had been to propose that the Community should embark on a policy of "deregulation" to stimulate its development as a "free trade and a free enterprise area." She was interested in the proposals of Arthur Cockfield, formerly the "prices commissioner" under Heath's government, whom she had sent to Brussels to become the senior British Commissioner under Jacques Delors: Lord Cockfield had produced a Commission White Paper entitled "Completing the Internal Market." This document identified nearly 300 measures by which the Community could by 1992 achieve the completion of its internal or "single market."

Ambush at Milan

Spinelli placed all his hopes on Mitterrand's intervention. But initially the French head of state kept his cards close to his chest. On the one hand, he was aware that expectations of a French success at the Milan Council were high. Accordingly, he had decided to take a long-term view, confiding to his advisor, Jacques Attali: "France's objective is to create a European Union in the long term; the task is now to define the substance and the stages. If we do not agree (at Milan) nothing will be done."[27] But, on the other hand he was informed that there were internal divisions in Germany's federal government and the reaction of the Chancellor's office was that the time was not yet ripe to consider alternatives to all the member states going forward together, particularly with respect to the occupying powers, that is, the United Kingdom as well as France.[28] It may well be that the political situation in the Soviet Union, where Gorbachev was to accede to the leadership a year later, weighed heavily with Chancellor Kohl, who had long combined what seemed to many to be, for his generation, the contradictory ambitions of achieving both European and German reunification—the latter requiring the consent of all four occupying powers. With United Kingdom resistance, Mitterrand felt that "ambitions had to be moderated." It was better to go for a bottom line that everyone could agree on. That bottom line was the Dooge Report and in particular, the completion of the Single Market.[29]

Although Spinelli recognized that the Dooge Report represented a severe dilution of his proposals, he did not reject it outright. Instead, he toured the European capitals with the President of the Institutional Committee, Mauro Ferri, urging an IGC as soon as possible, continuing to argue that it should work on the basis of his draft Treaty.[30] He identified Germany as the "weak spot" among the States whose support for the Draft Treaty was necessary: Kohl proposed postponement of the decision on the Committee's final report, with presentation only to the foreign ministers in March and it was not till June that it was presented to the European Council. Spinelli perceived that this delay was a danger for the Draft Treaty.[31] On 18 April 1985, the European Parliament enthusiastically approved a resolution moved by Spinelli insisting that it must be closely associated with the drafting of any new treaty and furthermore that the objections of the United Kingdom, Denmark, and Greece should not prevent other governments setting up the IGC.

At the same time Jacques Delors, as Commission president–designate, had also been touring the capitals, reaching the same conclusions as Mitterrand. He identified a new target for the Community process, thereby ending two decades of relative stagnation and meeting with the unanimous assent of the governments. The goal selected was the internal market project: the idea of building a truly barrier-free, Western Europe-wide market by the end of 1992. So Delors began his Commission Presidency, preparing, in collaboration with Arthur Cockfield and with great speed and energy, a very detailed White Paper on a program for ridding Europe of the nefarious non-tariff barriers that had clogged up the Common Market established in the 1960s, for presentation to the European Council in 1985.[32]

At the same time, in support of this policy Geoffrey Howe produced a report acknowledging that it would be impossible to make real progress toward the "Single Market" as long as the unanimity rule prevailed, allowing national vetoes, but he also argued that a new treaty would not be necessary to reduce the number of issues requiring unanimity. The Treaty of Rome could remain unchanged, but there should be a written "gentleman's agreement" that the Single Market could proceed as though the unanimity rule did not apply. Howe also proposed a greater degree of "political cooperation" on foreign policy and that, if necessary, the Council should be given a political secretariat.[33]

Two weeks after having seen the Howe proposal (Thatcher presented it to Kohl at Chequers) the Germans produced their own counter-proposals: a treaty between the Twelve to "mark a new stage in the progression toward the European Union" and to establish a common foreign and security policy. Then, just as the Milan Council approached, Mitterrand announced that he would support the German proposals, to transform it into a "Franco-German project": thus, a start would be made on the "construction of a political Europe," directed by the European Council, which would be flanked by a General Secretariat, dominated by the Ministries of Foreign Affairs, operating in an intergovernmental framework.[34] To get started there would need to be an increase in majority voting, and both Kohl and Mitterrand were determined that there should be an IGC to push through the necessary changes to the Treaties.

The fact that Mitterrand had abandoned the Draft Treaty was extremely disturbing for Spinelli, who underwent a major cancer operation on 22 May, which seriously weakened him throughout the summer and prevented him from traveling until October. Nevertheless, great expectations had accompanied the handover of the EEC presidency to Italy, beginning on 1 January 1985, considering the great faith in the European idea that Italians had always shown both at government (Bettino Craxi and Giulio Andreotti) and at parliamentary level.[35] At the Milan Summit, no less than 50,000 people from philo-European movements had gathered to form the first mass demonstration of the European people. On 28 July at Milan, to Thatcher's astonishment, but with the previous agreement of Mitterrand and Kohl, Craxi invoked the right of the Presidency to call a vote, a highly unorthodox move. An IGC was agreed by a vote of seven to three.[36]

The Single European Act

While this was encouraging, the IGC was based on the Commission's White Paper and the Dooge Committee report, not the Parliament's Draft Treaty. During the Single European Act negotiations, the European Parliament was kept at a distance from the top table. It was the Commission which played a central role in the 1985 IGC's talks. Jacques Delors, the secretary general Émile Noël and François Lamoureux, the institutional expert, used the meetings of Foreign ministers and experts to saturate the delegates with proposals which "helped define the agenda and dissuaded many governments from putting forward ideas of their own." All proposals were drafted by these three, without reference to other Commissioners.[37] With considerable subtlety, Delors steered the negotiations in his direction by carefully linking the United Kingdom objectives, notably the Single Market, to institutional reform. The 1992 program would require a considerable amount of legislative activity—297 pieces of Community legislation would have to be passed before the Single Market could become a reality—which in turn acted as a catalyst for a decisive move toward greater use of qualified-majority voting. To get what they wanted, the British would thus be forced to concede that which they least wanted, an extension of qualified majority voting (QMV).[38] Once the mass of paperwork had been distilled to its essentials, the substantive issues emerged. The first two were acceptable to the British: the completion of the Single Market based on Cockfield's White Paper which strengthened cooperation policy. Delors had also put forward chapters on environmental policy, research, and cohesion (the so-called structural funds providing regional aid). The British agreed to these chapters as they led to a modest extension in the role of the European Parliament. There would, however, be a price that Britain would have to pay for its Single Market: the final version included twelve policy areas which would now be subject to QMV, including all measures considered necessary to establish the "internal market." There were two other battles, one initiated by Cockfield's proposal (transformed from British Minister to European Commissioner) on the harmonization of value-added tax rates and the other, by Delors, on Economic and Monetary Union. At the Luxembourg Summit on 2 and 3 December 1985, a Franco-German initiative enabled Delors to include in the preamble of the new Treaty a commitment "to the progressive realization of Economic and Monetary Union."[39]

Reaction to the Treaty was generally downbeat. Spinelli declared that the result of all his efforts had been "only a miserable little mouse, which many suspect is a dead mouse."[40] The real significance of the Single Act, however, was conveyed by its title.

Although it would be presented as mainly dealing with the Single Market, it was in reality a further crucial step toward building a Single Europe. The need for greater liberalization in Europe, supported by German, Italian, Belgian and Dutch Christian Democrats, and British Conservatives, parties of the center-right which ruled most of Western Europe in the early 1980s, eventually extended Community competences by taking over from national governments the power to make laws in several important new policy areas, notably the environment.[41] Through the extension of qualified majority voting it added substantially to the supranational nature of the Community. There was also the knowledge that this first serious revision of the Treaty of Rome was intended to pave the way for a second treaty, much more ambitious in its scope. One clue to this had been Delors' insistence on that declaration of intent about "Economic and Monetary Union."[42]

Conclusion

Although many of Spinelli's proposals were too radical for national governments, the Treaty negotiated between 1984 and 1986 represented a milestone in the history of the European Community. In certain respects all this was a taste of what was to come with the 2004 EU Constitution. On 23 May 1986, Altiero Spinelli died in Rome in his eightieth year. His dream might not have been fully achieved, but his life's work was done.

Notes

1. Piero Graglia, *Altiero Spinelli* (Bologna: Il Mulino, 2008), 584–85.

2. Julian Priestley, *Six Battles That Shaped Europe's Parliament* (London: John Harper Publishing, 2008): 8–10.

3. Altiero Spinelli, *Discorsi al Parlamento europeo (1976–1986)* (Bologna: Il Mulino, 1987): 210–11.

4. Historical Archives of the European Union (HAEU) *Debates of the European Parliament*, Mr. Spinelli's speech during the sitting of 11 December 1979: 97.

5. Altiero Spinelli, *Discorsi al Parlamento europeo*: 209–13.

6. Altiero Spinelli, *Diario europeo* (Bologna: Il Mulino, 1992), vol. 3, annotation of 31-12-1977.

7. HAEU, Pier Virgilio Dastoli collection (PVD) 7th letter from Altiero Spinelli to Piet Haux, 11 September 1984.

8. Daniele Pasquinucci, *Europeismo e Democrazia, Altiero Spinelli e la sinistra europea (1950–1986)* (Bologna: Il Mulino, 2000): 329, notes 52 and 53.

9. Lucia Felli, *Il gioco delle parti: l'azione del gruppo socialista al parlamento europeo nella prima legislatura*, unpublished dissertation of the University of Florence, 1996: 150–61.

10. *Agence Europe*, Europe Documents no. 1166/1167, 6 August 1981

11. Cinzia Rognoni, "Spinelli's Action in the European Parliament: The Crocodile Club, the Institutional Commission, The Draft Treaty," in *The Federal Idea*, ed. Andrea Bosco (London: Lothian Foundation Press, 1992), vol. 2: 286–99; AHEU, PVD/8 "Historique de l'action constitutionnelle du Parlement européen et de l'initiative du Comité d'Action pour une Constitution européenne," June 1983.

12. Altiero Spinelli, *Diario europeo*, vol. 3, annotations of 14 February and 16 April 1984; Archives Nationales France (ANF) AG (4) PM 8/2, Pierre Morel (Diplomatic Adviser) to Jean-Louis Bianco a/s: "Entretiens avec M. Piet Dankert. Projet de Traité sur l'union européenne," 16 April 1984.

13. "Mitterrand à Strasbourg devant les Dix," *Dernières Nouvelles d'Alsace* May 25, 1984; HAEU, Altiero Spinelli collection (AS) 366 Working document, speech by François Mitterrand, President of the European Council.

14. Roland Dumas, *Affaires étrangères* 1 (Paris: Fayard, 2007): 210–11.

15. ANF. 5 AG (4) PM 12, Dépêche Agence France Presse, 21 February 1984.

16. *Ibid.*, PM13, Note de Claude Cheysson pour M. le Président, 30 December 1983.

17. *Ibid.*, PM 12, Note Direction Economique et Financière, Service de Coopération économique a/s: "Présidence française: réforme des institutions (Projet Spinelli)," December 1983.

18. Jean-Marie Palayret, "Spinelli, entre cellule carbonara et conseiller des princes. Impulsions et limites de la relance européenne dans le projet d'Union politique des années 80," in *Inventer l'Europe. Histoire nouvelle des groupes d'influence et des acteurs de l'Union européenne*, ed. Gérard Bossuat (Brussels: PIE Peter Lang, 2003): 355–82.

19. Christopher Booker and Richard North, *The Great Deception. The Secret History of the European Union* (London: Continuum, 2003): 208.

20. ANF, 5 AG (4) 13: Note de Pierre Morel pour le Président a/s "Mandat pour le Comité Dooge," 23 August 1984.

21. A memo issued by the "Spaak Ad Hoc Committee on Institutional Matters" (end of July 1984) stated clearly that "The formula of the new Treaty proposed by Altiero Spinelli has the advantage that it might achieve European Union among some of the Member States."

22. HAEU, AS 365, Note de la Direction générale des Commissions du Parlement européen a/s: "Comité ad hoc Spaak" (PE 91.631), 21 September 1984; ibid. PE 94.587, Provisional Report of the "Ad Hoc Committee on Institutional Matters," 12 December 1984.

23. Georges Saunier, "Prélude à la relance de l'Europe: le couple franco-allemand et les projets de relance communautaire vus de l'Hexagone," in *Le couple France -Allemagne et les institutions européennes*, ed. Marie-Thérèse Bitsch (Brussels: Bruylant, 2001: 464–85.

24. François Mitterrand, *Réflexions sur la politique extérieure de la France* (Paris: Fayard, 1985): 281.

25. ANF, 5 AG (4) PM 8-f.2, Note de Pierre Morel pour le Président a/s: "Comité Spaak, schéma de réflexion franco-allemand," 20 September 1984; Jacques Attali, *Verbatim* (Paris: Fayard, 1993), vol. 1: 1218, annotation of 29 April 1985.

26. HAEU, AS 365 (file PE94.598) "Note établissant un parallèle entre le rapport du Comité Dooge et le projet de Traité instituant l'Union européenne," 13 December 1984.

27. Jacques Attali, *Verbatim*, vol. 1:1215, annotation of 22 April 1985.

28. Pierre Favier and Michel Martin-Rolland, *La décennie Mitterrand, tome 2, Les épreuves (1984–1988)* (Paris: Seuil, 1991): 215.

29. ANF, 5 AG (4) EG 13 Note d'Elisabeth Guigou pour le Président a/s: "Votre rencontre avec le Chancelier Kohl: Que faire pour l'Europe?" 20 May 1985.

30. HAEU, PVD 8, Visit of On. Ferri to The Hague (2 May 1985), Brussels (5 May 1985), Copenhagen (9 May 1985).

31. Cinzia Rognoni, "Spinelli's action in the European: The Crocodile Club, the Institutional Commission, The Draft Treaty," in *The Federal Idea*, ed. Andrea Bosco (London:Lothian Foundation Press, 1992), vol. 2: 286–99.

32. Jacques Delors, *Mémoires* (Plon, Paris, 2003): 203–5.

33. Paul Sharp, *Thatcher's Diplomacy: The Revival of British Foreign Policy* (London: Macmillan,1999), 162–63; *Agence Europe*, bulletin no. 4078, 26 April 1985.

34. Jacques Attali, *Verbatim*, vol. 1: 1229–30, annotations of 10 and 13 May 1985.

35. Antonio Badini, "La presidenza italiana della CEE" in *Affari Esteri*, 68 (1985): 427–35.

36. Jean-Marie Palayret, "Visto da Parigi. La Francia, l'Italia e la costruzione europea durante la presidenza di François Mitterrand 1981–1991," in *L'Italia nella Costruzione europea. Un bilancio storico 1957–2007*, ed. Piero Craveri and Antonio Varsori (Milan: Franco Angeli, 2009): 431–54.

37. Booker and North: 220.

38. Delors: 208.

39. Jean-Marie Palayret, "The French Road to European Monetary Integration during the Maastricht Treaty Negotiations," in Stefania Baroncelli, Carlo Spagnolo, and Leila Talani, *Back to Maastricht. Obstacles to Constitutional Reform within the EU Treaty (1991–2007)*, ed. Stefania Baroncelli, Carlo Spagnolo, and Leila Talani (Cambridge: Cambridge Scholars Publishing, 2008): 242–64.

40. Altiero Spinelli, *Diario europeo*, vol. 2. 1216–7, annotations of 29 and 30 June 1985.

41. Piers Ludlow, "From Deadlock to Dynamism: the EC in the 1980s," in *Origins and Evolution of the European Union*, ed. Desmond Dinan (Oxford: Oxford University Press, 2006): 218–32.

42. Jean Deruyt, *L'Acte unique européen, Commentaire* (Brussels: Editions de l'université de Bruxelles, 1987), 77–85; HAEU, PVD 6, "Comptes rendus succincts des réunions de la Conférence des gouvernements des Etats membres," Luxembourg, 19–21 October 1985.

Conclusion

Altiero Spinelli and the Future of the European Union

Andrew Glencross

The dominant narrative of EU integration offers an overwhelmingly positive portrayal of the gradual edification of a new form of polity in the context of postwar reconstruction and reconciliation in Europe.[1] Yet the head scratching and hand wringing amongst Europe's political elites during the constitutional stasis that followed the rejection of the Constitutional Treaty, by French and Dutch voters, suggest a reevaluation of this narrative is more than warranted. As a staunch advocate of a fully federal form of unification that never materialized, Spinelli is perhaps an unlikely figure to draw upon in order to understand why the integration project has been buffeted of late. However, as a trenchant critic of the functionalist manner in which Europe's nation-states sought, after World War II, to leave behind the inherently flawed system of balance of power, he provides useful guidance for explaining the issues that continue to bedevil the EU system. This task is all the more necessary in a context of increased popular dissatisfaction with both the product and project of integration.[2] In order to understand his contemporary importance, it is first important to restate and draw together the central themes of Spinelli's intellectual and political endeavors that have been discussed in the preceding chapters.

Starting in the 1940s, Spinelli developed a critique of the functionalist variant of integration in order to vindicate the federal alternative. Of course, both these pro-European positions fundamentally share the hope that a supranational form of political authority would put an end to the cult of national sovereignty and the failed policy of balance of power this entailed. But whereas the functionalist position advocates an evolutionary form of integration based initially on a piecemeal functional pooling of government authority in the economic sphere, federalism seeks to effect this change immediately in the form of a constitutional revolution. Spinelli's argument in favor of the latter—a debate he contributed to throughout his life—was twofold. In part, it was historical, based on claiming that conditions in Europe were no less propitious than for many other eventually successful federations. But it was also based on the conceptual proposition that only federal constitutionalism could solve the problems of democratic authorization and accountability that integration raises.

Throughout his career as a thinker and political actor, therefore, Spinelli first tried to refute the starting premise of functionalism, namely that the time was not right for implementing a federal blueprint. Secondly he demonstrated that the alternative course to federalism produced various democratic shortcomings. Lastly, and as evinced by his design for a radical new treaty in 1984, he was highly skeptical that the performance per se of supranational government could establish the legitimacy of a new polity. *Pace* Haas' neo-functionalist theory that expected legitimacy to follow the successful performance of tasks by supranational authority, Spinelli's federalist theory claimed that such a transfer in authority could only be legitimated through a prior constitutional move sanctioned by Europe's citizens. Using these three themes to illuminate the EU constitutional debates of the past decade is the best way to evaluate the enduring worth of Spinelli's work in an integration process still fundamentally in flux.

The Conditions for Federalism in Europe

Despite a large volume of literature covering the travails of various types of federal states across time and contexts, there is no academic consensus over what ultimately causes federalism to prosper or else founder. This has not stopped many critics of a federally integrated Europe from claiming that the constituent parts of such a project are too heterogeneous—socially, economically, and politically—to be a success. Almost invariably such reflections make an analogy with the United States' federal system to determine what can be considered the preconditions for a federal polity on a continental scale. Perhaps the best exemplar of this tradition is Larry Siedentop, for whom a successful European federation presupposes the emulation of the

United States' three common cultural traits: a shared language, a common religion, and a legally trained political class.[3]

Such claims that Europe lacks the proper material for a viable federal union were well known to Spinelli, since this was the primary justification for pursuing functionalist integration. In response, he repeatedly pointed out that analogies with the United States overlooked the many doubts about the endurance of the federal constitution expressed by those living in the formative moments of the early republic. This critique of the tendency to write off the federal solution in Europe by relying on flawed teleological interpretations of American federalism is amply supported by recent international relations scholarship. With the end of the Cold War having liberated scholars from a dominant realist paradigm that understood the U.S. federal system as just another unit in the international system,[4] IR scholars have demonstrated the ongoing tensions in this supposed archetype of successful federalism. Not only did the "Philadelphian system," as Daniel Deudney calls it, tread a fine line in trying to "prevent simultaneously the emergence of hierarchy and anarchy,"[5] an experiment that ultimately failed given the Civil War. Moreover, the foreign relations of the federal republic, which owing to territorial expansion had a profound impact on the inner political workings, were for over a hundred years a struggle between imperial, national, and unionist visions of the federal system's engagement with the outside world.[6]

Returning to Europe, it is evident that, despite the conditions affecting the viability of federalism being perhaps no more precarious than those to be found in late eighteenth-century America, the political momentum for European federalism has faltered. The last federalist-minded president of the European Commission was Jacques Delors, whose tenure ended in 1994. Amongst national politicians, the generation of leaders since Mitterrand and Kohl—in particular those in France and Germany—have given little indication of an inclination toward a federal polity. Meanwhile, popular activism in favor of such an end goal has dwindled. Hence while the empirical evidence from comparative federalism and constitutionalism supports Spinelli's thesis that there is no universally appropriate time and set of conditions upon which to found a federal state, attempts to generate the momentum toward such a constitutional revolution seem to have come to naught in today's Europe. This seems a curious state of affairs given not only the existence of a quasi-federal legal system that recognizes the sovereign authority of European legislation[7] but also the attempt in 2005 to endow the EU with a constitutional foundation.

To explain this disjuncture between the successful institutionalization of integration and the reluctance to pursue an overtly federalist project, it is necessary to turn toward the growing popular frustrations with the EU. As Bartolini's chapter skillfully explained, this frustration is shared by both skeptics and enthusiasts of integration. On the one hand, skeptics feel the EU—having developed "by stealth"[8]—is already operating in practice as a federal straightjacket upon member-state autonomy and with little regard to explicit treaty safeguards of state sovereignty. On the other hand, Euro-enthusiasts are dissatisfied with the unwillingness to utilize explicitly the idiom of federalism as a way of legitimizing the supranational polity while also assuaging fears of inexorable interventionism and threatening homogenization.

Bartolini's analysis concurs with three fundamental factors that help explain further the absence of a federalist momentum. Firstly, the dispute between proponents and opponents of continued integration highlights Glyn Morgan's point that there is no ready consensus over what stage integration has reached and how its impact on the nation-state is to be understood.[9] Secondly, federalism itself has different connotations within Europe's national political cultures: the German perspective typically interprets such a system as a guarantor of sub-state autonomy, which is opposed by the British tradition that sees this as a cloak for abolishing nation-state prerogatives.[10] Finally, the demise of confederalism—the option that de Gaulle tried and failed to put into practice—as a genuine alternative institutional form of organizing inter-state cooperation in Europe[11] has removed an important rival concept from the debate over EU finality. Fabbrini's contribution to this volume showed the importance of a shared constitutional discourse in sustaining U.S. federalism over the ages in the face of myriad interpretations of constitutional meaning. Yet in the United States this common constitutional framework was historically dependent upon the prior negation of the Anti-Federalists' (advocates of a confederal republic) arguments against the U.S. Constitution. Paradoxically, therefore, Europe has set aside the purely confederal option of integration without gaining the ability to construct a shared constitutional language with which to understand and debate the dilemmas of integration today. In this sense, Spinelli's oft-repeated plea that the conditions are appropriate for a genuinely federal turn in European integration—even if true—continues to lack a receptive audience today.

Constitutionalism without Federalism: What Effects on Democracy?

The EU's constitutional architecture, as artfully detailed in this volume by Bruno de Witte, is a highly abstruse mechanism whose legal complexity is a product of a punctuated development over the course of various treaty revisions ever since the European Coal and Steel Community was created in 1951. The treaties apportion competences horizontally, amongst the EU institutions, as well as vertically, between the EU and its member states. But by placing a heavy emphasis on consensual decision making the institutional order strays greatly from the classic separation of powers between executive, legislative, and judicial powers. In particular, the European Commission combines a range of executive functions alongside a monopoly of legislative initiative in the first so-called pillar of policy issues, which it retains even though the Lisbon Treaty formally abolishes the pillar architecture. Moreover, by seeking to shield the pooling of sovereignty from possible future U-turns by turncoat member states seeking to renege on their earlier commitments, the treaty system places a very high barrier to the revision of policy goals enshrined in the treaties.

EU constitutionalism differs markedly, therefore, from the classic notion of constitutionalism as a means of restraining the exercise of political power. Instead, as Bartolini makes clear in this volume, the EU treaty system is designed to protect a set of predefined policy goals in addition to regulating relations between decision-making institutions. Hence the impact on democratic accountability is twofold. The emphasis on consensual decision making—the "community method" that mixes intergovernmentalism with supranationalism[12]—creates a "joint-decision trap," whereby significant policy decisions are commonly taken at the lowest common denominator level. This stymies effective policy responses to a range of issues, especially where certain interests are firmly entrenched in member state politics such as agriculture. In addition, the treaty protection afforded to substantive policy goals makes these almost impossible to revise—far harder than revising the constitution in an ordinary federal state—as the only possible opportunity is during a periodic intergovernmental conference on treaty revision. Since these are largely conducted as diplomatic affairs, they remain highly impervious to oversight and instruction from national parliaments and political parties, which are further hampered owing to the absence of proper coordination at a pan-European level. This problem of democratic mobilization explains why, already in 1984, Spinelli sought to galvanize European parliamentarians to create the momentum behind a constituent process to fundamentally revise the European political order on the basis of a single constitutional text. Of course, as Palayret's chapter reconstructing the strategy for passing the 1984 Draft Treaty demonstrates, Spinelli was also a realist who courted then French President François Mitterrand in the hope of gaining a prominent national sponsor for this European endeavor.

The 1984 Draft Treaty produced by the European Parliament represents the high-water mark of this institution's engagement with a federalist project of integration. However, as Ponzano noted in his contribution, the legacy of Spinelli's advocacy of a constituent process did not pass away with the demise of this short-lived flirtation with a federal constitution. Rather, the recent attempt to expand participation in the process of treaty reform through the convention method is a testament to the enduring desire to generate a European constitutional moment to reconfigure political authority on the basis of a pan-European popular mandate. The idea of calling a special convention drawing its representatives from the member states, civil society, and European institutions was put into practice to devise a Charter of Fundamental Rights and Freedoms in 2000 and again three years later to discuss the political finality of the integration project. Given the failure of what subsequently emerged—the Constitutional Treaty, replaced after the referendum failures in France and the Netherlands by a hastily redrawn treaty, ratified on 13 December 2007 in Lisbon by the usual technique of an intergovernmental conference—it is evident that the problem of Europe's absent constituent power remains unresolved to this day. This still does not mean, however, that attempts to set in motion a constituent process that would democratize the EU ended with Spinelli's Draft Treaty of 1984.

One attempted solution to the problem of having a constituent power give sanction to supranationalism is the holding of national referendums on treaty revision. Yet since this use of direct democracy in France and the Netherlands (as well as Ireland for the later Lisbon Treaty) was responsible for the defenestration of the Constitutional Treaty, this appears a particularly fickle device for generating foundational legitimacy for the integration project. Of course, the thorny history of national referendums has led to the call, from some quarters, for the introduction of pan-European votes, requiring the dual majority principle of states and citizens that is found in Swiss referendums on constitutional change.[13] Spinelli would no doubt have approved of this resort to majoritarianism as it implies a significant shift away from the primacy of the confederal principle of state representation to the federal representation of citizens qua European citizens. Nonetheless, the prospects at present for such a drastic transformation appear unpromising as European elites are struggling to close the lid on the Pandora's box of referendums even at the national level as a result of the near-decade long complications these have caused the integration process.

However, popular mobilization behind treaty revision is not the only issue that still troubles the EU's democratic legitimacy. EU treaties are inevitably characterized by a certain degree of "incomplete contracting."[14] That is, as much as they define substantive policy goals and decision-making procedures, they cannot fully specify *ex ante* all the conditions under which the appropriate decision-making rules will be followed in each set of policy areas. The result is the complex legal ambiguity, pointed out in de Witte's chapter, which increasingly leads the European Court of Justice (ECJ) to pronounce upon vexing problems of horizontal and vertical separation of powers. This is a common enough occurrence in federal systems, as demonstrated by John Dewey's famous proposition that federalism is synonymous with legalism. The democratic anxiety peculiar to the EU though is that the judicial body tasked with cutting the Gordian knot of legal complexity to adjudicate responsibility for policy making is seemingly far too removed from considerations of wider public preferences. The reason for this fear is that while the ECJ has the responsibilities of a federal supreme court the absence of a federal political structure makes it harder for elected representatives to respond to or at least shape the context of fundamental jurisprudence.

For instance, the role of the U.S. Supreme Court as final arbiter of the constitution was fully accepted after the Civil War[15] and Roosevelt's tussle with the justices during the New Deal made it clear that their jurisprudence in the final instance had to take a cue from public opinion as expressed in the electoral mandate of the president. By contrast, the ECJ functions in a rather different political and institutional environment. The only way member states can respond to a significant jurisprudential interpretation of the EU treaties is by redrafting those very treaties, a move that must overcome a threshold of veto-players even more demanding than that required to revise the U.S. Constitution. Moreover, as a fiduciary institution rather than a mere agent of the contracting states, the ECJ is supposed to oversee respect for the treaties so as to render states' commitments credible.[16] Yet in the absence of a pan-European public sphere, close media scrutiny, and directly elected representatives wielding strong, European-level legislative mandates, there is a less well-defined "strategic space"[17] for politics to set the limits on the judicial impact on EU policy making.

As an important agenda-setter in the integration process, the ECJ's disconnection from political representation and the broader European public sphere is thus highly problematic from the perspective of democratic accountability. The potential of the Court to impinge on issues dear to voters in certain member states was evinced in 1991 as a result of the ECJ's willingness to hear a case (*Society for the Protection of Unborn Children Ireland Ltd. v. Grogan*) concerning the distribution in Ireland of information leaflets about UK abortion clinics. The case was heard on the grounds that abortion was a service and thus came under the remit of EU legislation on free movement of services.

The verdict rendered in this case—which upheld Ireland's right to restrict information about legal abortions performed in the United Kingdom—did nothing to dismantle the legal apparatus prohibiting abortion in Ireland. Nevertheless, the outcry surrounding the notion that the ECJ was potentially competent over such questions led to the insertion into the Maastricht Treaty of a protocol guaranteeing Irish autonomy over abortion policy.

The legal status of this protocol remains unclear to this day, as does the United Kingdom's recent opt-out—contained in the Lisbon Treaty—from the legal effects of the Charter of Fundamental Rights and Freedoms, rights set to become binding when implementing any EU legislation. In this way, the ECJ is increasingly tasked with resolving the problems of legal interpretation that arise from treaties whose ambiguity is the result of having to find taxing compromises between intergovernmentalists and supranationalists. Yet at the same time, the Court operates without the buttress of solid federal mechanisms for representing popular sovereignty—either to legislate in the wake of jurisprudence or to indicate political sentiment before the Court renders a verdict. This is a situation, as Glencross's chapter argues, reminiscent of the antebellum United States, a period when the supremacy of the Supreme Court was repeatedly called into question,[18] while the judicial attempt to settle the major political issue of the day, slavery, in the *Dred Scott* decision precipitated the demise of the union. If the analogy holds, it suggests the integration process may be confronted in the future by stark competence disputes in which ECJ rulings, necessary to prevent institutional blockage amidst increasing legal complexity, could be explosive.

Thus the creation of a novel form of constitutionalism without responsive mechanisms for representing popular sovereignty renders the solution of competence and policy disputes difficult. In particular, the EU's political institutions will find it hard to contain the fallout from controversial jurisprudence as the ECJ is tasked to resolve legal ambiguity. Spinelli himself originally failed to anticipate the ECJ's ability to restrain member-state sovereignty through supremacy and direct effect, thinking that the Court would be an inadequate substitute for a formal surrender of nation-state sovereignty to a federal constitution. Nevertheless, he was highly sensitive to the EU's fundamental weakness of relying on indirect representation when legality clashed with legitimacy. Devoid of federal mechanisms of popular legitimacy, he argued that the neo-functionalist institutional blueprint could not prevail by counting on legality alone. Consequently, he also disbelieved that neo-functionalist performance could establish its own form of *ex post* legitimacy, a question that still remains to be answered today.

Establishing Supranational Legitimacy through Institutional Performance?

The functionalist program for refounding the nature of governance away from national territorial sovereignty is inextricably tied to the premise that institutional performance is the *fons et origo* of political legitimacy in the modern age. This has its source in David Mitrany's paean to the Tennessee Valley Authority as an extra-constitutional rupture with classic separation of powers for the sake of serving the common good according to the precept that governmental form must follow function.[19] It was this line of thinking that inspired the neo-functionalist vision of European integration, with the mantra that having left behind state sovereignty "authority will be judged in terms of its effectiveness in coping with complexly linked issues on the European agenda."[20] The evidence from over fifty years of integration, however, suggests that Spinelli's reservations about the ability of the functionalist path of integration to generate legitimacy at the expense of the nation-state were largely well founded.

Spinelli was no believer in relying upon a permissive consensus amongst Europe's citizens to undergird the integration process in the context of assumed spillover effects leading to ever closer union. Instead, he problematized why citizens would be prepared to accept such transfers of authority in the first place. In order for this reconfiguration of government to be legitimate, he originally advocated the convocation of a constituent assembly, drawing on specially elected national representatives, to usher in a federal constitution. However, as Ponzano's chapter shows, the introduction of direct elections for European parliamentarians later persuaded Spinelli that the European Parliament could now play this instigating role. Of course, both scenarios presupposed the possibility of generating continent-wide support in favor of federalism, at least amongst Europe's political elites. Indeed, in his early work he even went so far as to claim that the most important step was to persuade these elites to accept a federal revolution because a federation could always be democratized subsequently whereas the abandonment of state sovereignty was a necessary and sufficient condition for integration.[21]

Nevertheless, integration has undoubtedly progressed steadily without recourse to an overt and incontrovertible surrender of national sovereignty to a federal constitutional system. Moreover, as discussed above, the federalist tendencies of current European elites are lukewarm at best. This means the EU is an excellent test case for observing the extent to which institutional performance can generate legitimacy, what Scharpf has called "output legitimacy."[22] This preoccupation with popular perceptions of performance has permeated EU institutions since the early 1970s. It was at this time, when the enlargement of the then European Economic Community led to greater scrutiny of the institutions of integration, that the *Eurobarometer* polling organization was created to survey national publics' attitudes to European institutions. In addition, both turnout and voter preferences in European parliamentary elections as well as a host of ad hoc national referendums on integration issues have been interpreted as bellwethers of public perceptions of EU legitimacy.

Eurobarometer's polls have for a long time revealed marked national differences over support for the EU between net recipients of structural and regional aid as compared with net creditors.[23] These indicate a clear correlation between perceived national economic benefits of integration and support for EU institutions. Similarly, the degree of trust expressed in these supranational institutions is greater the more cynical citizens are about political and judicial institutions in their own countries, a phenomenon particularly true of certain Eastern and Central European member states. However such indicators are probably poor proxies for gauging political legitimacy in a classic Weberian sense as they take place in a context devoid of high stakes political decision making. This is why European parliamentary elections and national referendum votes are typically seen as more telling indicators of citizen satisfaction with the project and product of integration. Indeed, these electoral moments have engendered European-level crises of legitimacy, notably in the panicked and downright dumbfounded reactions that have accompanied recent referendum defeats of proposed treaty reform.

Judged in light of the periodic failure of national publics to support referendums on treaty reform, EU institutions have clearly struggled to establish legitimacy through policy effectiveness. This can be seen by contrasting national debates in applicant states with those in long-standing member states. In the former, such as Switzerland for instance, voters have rejected EU accession largely as an expression of the perceived incompatibility of national identity with EU membership.[24] However, in those existing member states where referendums on treaty reform have failed—Ireland, Denmark, France and the Netherlands—the cause has mostly been attributed to dissatisfaction with current and expected future policy outcomes rather than an identity-based grievance. In this context of contested EU policy making and institution building, the attempt to furnish a constitution-like founding text no doubt gave a further turn of the screw to citizens' dissatisfaction with certain features of integration, even if these differed between countries. Thus it appears that the neo-functionalist project has encountered precisely the legitimacy problem Spinelli anticipated, namely that new-fangled institutions of governance will find it difficult to accrue legitimacy in the absence of an original popular mandate to sanction such institutional changes.

The existence of this legitimacy problem does not necessarily imply that the federal model is the only warranted solution to the EU's current woes. For a start, it may just be that coordination problems across a Council of Ministers now numbering twenty-seven and an increasingly potent European Parliament are hampering policy performance. It is precisely to counter such weaknesses that one prominent scholar of integration has advocated the need for "politicizing" the EU policy process. The aim of this politicization advocated by Simon Hix is to ensure that EU decision making reflects better at the European level the left-right cleavage that pertains within national politics by increasing the dosage of majoritarianism in the EU institutions. However, as Bartolini's contribution makes abundantly clear, there is no *a priori* reason why such coordinated partisanship would be welcomed as a legitimate constitutive change in the nature of the EU polity by voters already diffident toward a range of EU policies. In this fashion, politicization is redolent of federalism by the backdoor—exactly the sort of disingenuous political maneuvering Spinelli associated with neo-functionalists.

Conclusion

The successful Irish referendum re-vote on the Lisbon Treaty in October 2009 put an end to a fraught process of institutional reform intended to democratize EU decision making, to create a clearer competence catalogue, and to ensure institutional effectiveness in the wake of a major expansion in member states. The process itself lasted nearly a decade; the Laeken Declaration that originally called for an intergovernmental conference to study how to render the EU more democratic, effective and transparent dates back to 15 December 2001. On all three counts, the Lisbon Treaty has made some progress. But as the contributors to this volume have discussed in detail the changes contained in the new treaty are certainly insufficient to end popular contestation over the EU's legitimacy and its policy effectiveness. Some of this contestation surfaced in the referendum rejections in France, the Netherlands, and Ireland that punctuated the process of treaty reform. It is also apparent in the increasing turn, across the EU, toward anti-EU and populist parties both in European parliamentary elections as well as within domestic politics. In the midst of the greatest economic turmoil in a generation, EU member states have also battled to stifle atavistic instincts of protectionism, efforts which even if successful are indicative of the residual presence of national favoritism despite over fifty years of integration. In such circumstances, the constitutional future of the EU is obviously still uncertain.

The relevance of Altiero Spinelli to understanding what is at stake in this contested future is, as this concluding chapter has emphasized, not merely as a guide to what a federal Europe should look like. Rather, by questioning the assumptions that Europe lacks the proper conditions for federalism, that constitutionalism can function adequately without federal political representation or that policy effectiveness is sufficient to generate institutional legitimacy, Spinelli's thought has much to contribute to the debate over the EU's future. This is not to undermine the importance of his work and writings in providing a federalist vision for imagining a more fully integrated Europe. However, the purpose of this volume has been to show that whatever the merits of his answer to Europe's constitutional dilemma, the awkward questions he raised about European integration are still those most in need of an answer. The Lisbon Treaty may go some way to furnishing these but the EU constitutional dialogue is far from over, and until it is Spinelli will continue to illuminate a course where the straightforward pathway has not so much been lost as rather never existed to begin with.

Notes

1. Mark Gilbert, "Narrating the Process: Questioning the Progressive Story of European Integration," *Journal of Common Market Studies* 46, no. 3 (June 2008): 641–62.

2. Simon Hix, *What's Wrong with the European Union and How to Fix It?* (Oxford: Polity, 2008).

3. Larry Siedentop, *Democracy in Europe* (London: Allen Lane, 2000).

4. See for instance Hans Morgenthau, *Politics Among Nations. The Struggle for Power and Peace* (New York: Alfred Knopf, 1985).

5. Daniel Deudney, "The Philadelphian State System: Sovereignty, Arms Control, and Balance of Power in the American State System," *International Organization* 49, no. 2 (March 1995): 191–229, 208.

6. David C. Hendrickson, *Union, Nation or Empire: The American Debate over International Relations, 1789–1941* (Lawrence: University of Kansas Press, 2008).

7. Leslie F. Goldstein, *Constituting Federal Sovereignty: The European Union in Comparative Context* (Baltimore: Johns Hopkins University Press, 2001).

8. Giandomenico Majone, *Dilemmas of European Integration: The Ambiguities and Pitfalls of Integration by Stealth* (Oxford: Oxford University Press, 2005).

9. Glyn Morgan, *The Idea of a European Superstate: Public Justification and European Integration* (Princeton: Princeton University Press, 2005).

10. Renaud Dehousse, "We the States: Why the Anti-Federalists Won," in Nicolas Jabko and Craig Parsons, eds., *With Us or Against US? European Trends in American Perspective* (New York: Oxford University Press, 2005): 105–21.

11. Craig Parsons A *Certain Idea of Europe* (Ithaca, NY: Cornell University Press, 2003).

12. Majone, *Dilemmas*.

13. Andreas Auer, "National Referendums in the Process of European Integration: Time for a Change," in Anneli Albi and Jacques Ziller, eds., *The European Constitution and National Constitutions: Ratification and Beyond.* (The Hague: Kluwer Law International, 2008): 261–72.

14. Alexander Cooley and Hendrik Spruyt, *Contracting States: Sovereign Transfers in International Relations* (Princeton: Princeton University Press, 2009).

15. Forrest McDonald, *States' Rights and the Union: Imperium in Imperio, 1776–1876* (Lawrence: University of Kansas Press, 2000).

16. Giandomenico Majone, "Two Logics of Delegation: Agency and Fiduciary Relations in EU Governance," *European Union Politics* 2, no. 1 (February 2001): 103–22.

17. Richard H. Steinberg "Judicial Lawmaking at the WTO: Discursive, Constitutional and Political Constraints," *American Journal of International Law* 98, no. 2 (April 2004): 247–75, 263–64.

18. Goldstein, *Constituting Federal Sovereignty*.

19. David Mitrany, *A Working Peace System: An Argument for the Functional Development of International Organization* (London: Royal Institute of International Affairs, 1943): 21–23.

20. Ernst Haas, *The Obsolescence of Regional Integration Theory*, University of California, Institute of International Studies, Research Series, no. 25 (Berkeley, 1975): 79.

21. Altiero Spinelli, *Europa Terza Forza. Politica estera e difesa comune negli anni della guerra fredda. Scritti 1947–1954* (Bologna : Il Mulino, 2000): 9.

22. Fritz Scharpf, *Governing in Europe* (Oxford: Oxford University Press, 1999).

23. Lauren McLaren, *Identity, Interests and Attitudes to European Integration* (Basingstoke: Palgrave, 2006).

24. Thomas Christin and Alexander H. Trechsel, "Joining the EU? Explaining Public Opinion in Switzerland," *European Union Politics* 3, no. 4 (December 2002): 415–43.

Bibliography

Ackerman, Bruce. *We the People: Foundations*. Cambridge, Mass.: Harvard University Press, 1991.

Adler-Nissen, Rebecca. "Organized Duplicity? When States Opt Out of the European Union." Pp. 81–103 in *Sovereignty Games: Instrumentalizing State Sovereignty in a European and Global Context*. Edited by Rebecca Adler-Nissen and Thomas Gammeltoft-Hansen. New York: Palgrave, 2008.

Auer, Andreas. "National Referendums in the Process of European Integration: Time for a Change." Pp. 261–72 in *The European Constitution and National Constitutions: Ratification and Beyond*. Edited by Anneli Albi and Jacques Ziller. The Hague: Kluwer Law International, 2008.

Badini, Antonio. "La presidenza italiana della CEE." *Affari Esteri* 68 (1985): 427–35.

Baker, Leonard. *John Marshall: A Life in Law*. New York: Macmillan, 1974.

Bartolini, Stefano. *Restructuring Europe: Centre Formation, System Building, and Political Structuring Between the Nation State and the European Union*. Oxford: Oxford University Press, 2005.

Beard, Charles A., ed. *The Enduring Federalist*. New York: Frederick Ungar Publishing Co., 1948.

Beer, Samuel H. *To Make a Nation: The Rediscovery of American Federalism*. Cambridge, Mass.: Harvard University Press, 1993.

Bensel, Richard F. *Sectionalism and American Political Development: 1880–1980*. Madison: University of Wisconsin Press, 1987.

Bernstein, Richard B. *Amending America: If We Love the Constitution So Much, Why Do We Keep Trying to Change It?* Lawrence: University Press of Kansas, 1995.

Bleckmann, Albert. "Die Einheit der Europäischen Gemeinschaftsrechtsordnung. Einheit oder Mehrheit der Europäischen Gemeinschaften." *Europarecht* 13 (1978): 95–104.

Blondel, Jean. "Il modello svizzero: un futuro per l'Europa." *Rivista italiana di scienza politica* 28, no. 2 (1998): 203–27.

Blondel, Jean. "Formation, Life, and Responsibility of the European Executive." Paper presented at the University of Catania, workshop on "Democrazie ed Elezioni nell'Unione Europea," May 1999.

Bogdandy, Armin von. "The European Union as a Supranational Federation: A Conceptual Attempt in the Light of the Amsterdam Treaty." *Columbia Journal of European Law* 6 (2000): 27–54.

Bogdandy, Armin von, and Claus D. Ehlermann. "Consolidation of European Treaties: Feasibility, Costs and Benefits." *Common Market Law Review* 33, no. 6 (1996): 1107–109.

Booker, Christopher, and Richard North. *The Great Deception: The Secret History of the European Union*. London: Continuum, 2003.

Bribosia, Hervé. "De la simplification des traités au traité constitutionnel." Pp. 195–202 in *Genèse et destinée de la Constitution européenne*. Edited by Giuliano Amato, Hervé Bribosia, and Bruno de Witte. Bruxelles: Bruylant, 2007.

Burgess, Michael. *Federalism and European Union: The Building of Europe, 1950–2000*. London: Routledge, 2002.

Calleo, David P. *Rethinking Europe's Future*. Princeton: Princeton University Press, 2001.

Capotorti, Francesco et al. *The European Union Treaty: Commentary on the Draft Adopted by the EP on 14 February 1984*. Oxford: Oxford University Press, 1986.

Cappelletti, Mauro, Monica Seccombe, and Joseph H. H. Weiler, eds. *Integration Through Law: Europe and the American Federal Experience* 1, no. 1. Berlin: De Gruyter, 1986.

Christiansen, Thomas, and Christine Reh. *Constitutionalizing the European Union*. New York: Palgrave Macmillan, 2009.

Christin, Thomas, and Alexander H. Trechsel. "Joining the EU? Explaining Public Opinion in Switzerland," *European Union Politics* 3, no. 4 (December 2002): 415–43.

Cloos, Jim, Gaston Reinesch, Daniel Vignes, and Joseph Weyland. *Le Traité de Maastricht: Genèse, analyse, commentaires*. Bruxelles: Bruylant, 1993.

Cooley, Alexander, and Hendrik Spruyt. *Contracting States: Sovereign Transfers in International Relations*. Princeton: Princeton University Press, 2009.

Corbett, Richard. *The European Parliament's Role in Closer EU Integration*. Basingstoke: Palgrave, 1998.

Coultrap, John. "From Parliamentarism to Pluralism: Models of Democracy and the European Union's 'Democratic Deficit,'" *Journal of Theoretical Politics* 11, no. 1 (1999): 107–35.

Council of the European Union. *Presidency Conclusions*, Brussels, 21–22 June 2009, 11177/1/07 REV 1.

Craig, Paul, and Gráinne de Búrca, eds. *The Evolution of EU Law*. Oxford: Oxford University Press, 1999.
Curtin, Deirdre. "Emerging institutional parameters and organised difference in the European Union." Pp. 351–54 in *The Many Faces of Differentiation in EU Law*. Edited by Bruno de Witte, Dieter Hanf, and Ellen Vos. Antwerp: Intersentia, 2001.
———. "The Constitutional Structure of the Union: A Europe of Bits and Pieces," *Common Market Law Review* 30, no. 1 (1993): 17–70.
Curtin, Deirdre, and Ige Dekker. "The EU as a 'Layered' International Organization: Institutional Unity in Disguise." Pp. 154–89 in *The Evolution of EU Law*. Edited by Paul Craig and Gráinne de Búrca. Oxford: Oxford University Press, 1999.
Curtin, Deirdre, and Alfred E. Kellerman. *The EU Constitution: The Best Way Forward?* The Hague: Asser Press, 2006.
Dahl, Robert A. *A Preface to Democratic Theory* (expanded edition). New Haven, Conn.: Yale University Press, 2006
———. *How Democratic Is the American Constitution?* New Haven, Conn.: Yale University Press, 2001.
Dehousse, Renaud. "We the States: Why the Anti-Federalists Won." Pp. 105–21 in *With Us or Against US? European Trends in American Perspective*. Edited by Nicolas Jabko and Craig Parsons. New York: Oxford University Press, 2005.
Derthick, Martha. *Keeping the Compound Republic: Essays on Federalism*. Washington, D.C.: Brookings Institution, 2001.
De Ruyt, Jean. *L'Acte unique européen*. Brussels: Editions de l'université de Bruxelles, 1987.
Deudney, Daniel H. *Bounding Power: Republican Security Theory From the Polis to the Global Village*. Princeton, NJ: Princeton University Press, 2007.
———. "The Philadelphian State System: Sovereignty, Arms Control, and Balance of Power in the American State System." *International Organization* 49, no. 2 (March 1995): 191–229.
De Witte, Bruno. "Sources of Law and Law-Making in the Lisbon Treaty." Discussion paper presented at the conference "The Lisbon Treaty and the Future of the European Constitution," Florence, European University Institute, 11–12 April 2008.
———, ed. *Ten Reflections on the Constitutional Treaty for Europe*. Fiesole, Florence, EUI, Robert Schuman Centre, 2003.
———. "The Closest Thing to a Constitutional Conversation in Europe: The Semi-Permanent Treaty Revision Process." Pp. 39–57 in *Convergence and Divergence in European Public Law*. Edited by Paul Beaumont, Carole Lyons, and Neil Walker. Oxford: Hart, 2002.
———. "Direct Effect, Supremacy, and the Nature of Legal Order." Pp. 177–213 in *The Evolution of EU Law*, edited by Paul Craig and Gráinne de Búrca. Oxford: Oxford University Press, 1999.
———. "The Pillar Structure and the Nature of the European Union: Greek Temple or French Gothic Cathedral?" Pp, 56–85 in *The European Union after Amsterdam*.

Edited by Ton Heukels, Niels Blokker, and Marcel Brus. The Hague: Kluwer Law International, 1998.

Dinan, Desmond. *Ever Closer Union: An Introduction to European Integration*. New York: Palgrave Macmillan, 2005.

Dumas, Roland. *Affaires étrangères*. Paris: Fayard, 2007.

Elazar, Daniel J. "The United States and the European Union: Models of Their Epochs." Pp. 31–53 in *The Federal Vision and Levels of Governance in the US and in the EU*. Edited by Kalypso Nicolaïdis and Robert Howse. Oxford: Oxford University Press, 2001.

———. *The American Mosaic: The Impact of Space, Time, and Culture on American Politics*. Boulder, Colo.: Westview Press, 1994.

———. *The American Constitutional Tradition*. Lincoln: University of Nebraska Press, 1988.

———. "Constitution-Making: The Pre-eminently Political Act." Pp. 232–48 in *Redesigning the State: The Politics of Constitutional Change in Industrial Nations*. Edited by Keith G. Banting and Robert Simeon. Toronto: University of Toronto Press, 1985.

Elster, Jon. "Ways of Constitution-Making." Pp. 123–42 in *Democracy's Victory and Crisis*. Edited by Axel Hadenius. Cambridge: Cambridge University Press, 1997.

Epstein, Leon D. *Political Parties in the American Mold*. Madison: University of Wisconsin Press, 1986.

Erikson, Erik O., John E. Fossum, and A. J. Menéndez, eds. *Developing a Constitution for Europe*. London: Routledge 2004.

European Council. *Declaration on the Future of the European Union*. Laeken, 15 December 2001.

European Council. *Intergovernmental Conference on the Institutional Reform of the European Union*. Nice, 7–11 December 2000.

European Union. *Consolidated Version of the Treaty on the European Union*. Official Journal C 115, 9 May 2008.

European Union. *Treaty Establishing a Constitution for Europe*. Official Journal of the European Union, C 310, 47, 16 December 2004.

Everling, Ulrich. "From European Communities to European Union—by Convergence to Consistency." Pp. 139–58 in *European Integration and International Coordination. Studies in Transnational Law in Honour of Claus-Dieter Ehlermann*. Edited by Armin von Bogdandy, Paul Mavroidis, and Yves Mény. The Hague: Kluwer Law International, 2002.

Everson, Michelle, and Julia Eisner. *The Making of a European Constitution. Judges and Law Beyond Constitutive Power*. London: Routledge, 2007.

Fabbrini, Sergio. *Politica comparata. Introduzione alle democrazie contemporanee*. Roma/Bari: Laterza, 2008.

———. "The Constitutionalisation of a Compound Democracy: Comparing the European Union with the American Experience." *conWEB—webpapers on Con-*

stitutionalism and Governance beyond the State, no. 3 (2008) www.bath.ac.uk/esml/conWEB (accessed on August 22, 2010).

———. *America and Its Critics. Virtues and Vices of the Democratic Hyperpower*. Cambridge: Polity Press, 2008.

———. *Compound Democracies: Why the United States and Europe Are Becoming Similar*. Oxford: Oxford University Press, 2007.

———. "Madison in Brussels: The EU and the U.S. as Compound Democracies." *European Political Science* 4, no. 2 (2005): 188–98.

———. "Transatlantic Constitutionalism: Comparing the U.S. and the EU." Paper presented at the Transatlantic Studies Conference, University of Dundee, Scotland, 8–11 July 2002.

Farrand, Max. *The Records of the Federal Convention of 1787*. New Haven, Conn.: Yale University Press, 1996.

Favier, Pierre, and Michel Martin-Rolland. *La décennie Mitterrand, tome 2: Les épreuves (1984–1988)*. Paris: Seuil, 1991.

Felli, Lucia. *Il gioco delle parti: l'azione del gruppo socialista al parlamento europeo nella prima legislature*. Unpublished doctoral dissertation of the University of Florence, 1996.

Follesdal, Andreas, and Simon Hix. "Why There Is a Democratic Deficit in the EU: A Response to Majone and Moravcsik." *European Governance Papers* (EUROGOV) No. C-05-02, 2005.

Ford, Lacy K., Jr. "Inventing the Concurrent Majority: Madison, Calhoun, and the Problem of Majoritarianism in American Political Thought." *Journal of Southern History* 60, no. 1 (February 1944): 19–58.

Forsyth, Murray. *Unions of States. The Theory and Practice of Confederation*. New York: Leicester University Press, 1981.

Garton Ash, Timothy. *Free World. America: Europe, and the Surprising Future of the West*. New York: Random House, 2004.

Geddes, Andrew. *The European Union and British Politics*. New York: Palgrave Macmillan, 2004.

Gilbert, Mark. *Surpassing Realism. The Politics of European Integration Since 1945*. Lanham, Md.: Rowman & Littlefield, 2003.

Gilbert, Mark. "Narrating the Process: Questioning the Progressive Story of European Integration." *Journal of Common Market Studies* 46, no. 3 (June 2008): 641–62.

Glencross, Andrew. "Altiero Spinelli and the Idea of the U.S. Constitution as a Model for Europe: The Promises and Pitfalls of an Analogy." *Journal of Common Market Studies* 47, no. 2 (2009): 287–307.

Glencross, Andrew. *What Makes the EU Viable? European Integration in the Light of the Antebellum U.S. Experience*. New York: Palgrave Macmillan, 2009.

Goldstein, Leslie F. *Constituting Federal Sovereignty: The European Union in Comparative Context*. Baltimore: Johns Hopkins University Press, 2001.

Graglia, Piero S. *Altiero Spinelli*. Bologna: Il Mulino, 2008.

Haas, Ernst. *The Obsolescence of Regional Integration Theory*. University of California, Institute of International Studies, Research Series, no. 25 (1975).

Hamilton, Alexander et al. *The Federalist*. Cambridge: Cambridge University Press, 2003.

Hanf, Dieter. "Flexibility Clauses in the Founding Treaties, from Rome to Nice." Pp. 3–26 in *The Many Faces of Differentiation in EU Law*. Edited by Bruno de Witte et al. New York: Intersentia, 2001.

Hendrickson, David C. "Of Power and Providence." *Policy Review*, no. 135 (2006): 1–10.

———. *Peace Pact: The Lost World of the American Founding*. Lawrence: University Press of Kansas, 2003.

Héritier, Adrienne. "Elements of Democratic Legitimation in Europe: An Alternative Perspective." *Journal of European Public Policy* 6, no. 2 (June 1999): 269–82.

Hix, Simon. *What's Wrong with the European Union and How to Fix It*. Oxford: Polity, 2008.

———. "Why the EU Needs (Left-Right) Politics: Policy Reform and Accountability Are Impossible Without It." Paper for *Notre Europe*, Paris, 2006.

———. *The Political System of the European Union*. 2nd ed. New York: Palgrave Macmillan, 2005.

Ikenberry, G. John. *After Victory: Institutions, Strategic Restraints, and the Rebuilding of Order After Major Wars*. Princeton: Princeton University Press, 2000.

Jabko, Nicolas, and Craig Parsons, eds. *With Us or Against US? European Trends in American Perspective*. Oxford: Oxford University Press, 2005.

Jacqué, Jean-Paul. "La simplification et la consolidation des traités." *Revue trimestrielle de droit européen* 33, no. 4 (1997): 902–13.

Judt, Tony. *Postwar: A History of Europe Since 1945*. London: Penguin Books, 2005.

Jupille, Joseph, and James A. Caporaso. "Institutionalism and the European Union: Beyond Comparative Politics and International Relations." *Annual Review of Political Science* 2 (1999): 429–44.

Kernell, Samuel, ed. *James Madison: The Theory and Practice of Republican Government*. Palo Alto, Calif.: Stanford University Press, 2003.

King, Anthony. *The English Constitution*. Oxford: Oxford University Press, 2009.

Kriesi, Hans-Peter, and Alexander H. Trechsel. *The Politics of Switzerland: Continuity and Change in a Consensus Democracy*. Cambridge: Cambridge University Press, 2008.

Laursen, Finn, and Sophie Vanhoonacker. *The Intergovernmental Conference on Political Union*. Maastricht: European Institute of Public Administration, 2000.

Lenaerts, Koen, and Piet van Nuffel. *Constitutional Law of the European Union*. London: Thomson/Sweet & Maxwell, 2005.

Lepsius, M. Rainer "Integrazione economic-politica e pluralità culturale." *Il Mulino Europa* 2 (February 1997): 3–18.

Lijphart, Arend. *Patterns of Democracy: Government Forms and Performance in Thirty-Six Countries*. New Haven, Conn.: Yale University Press, 1999.

Lindberg, Leon N. *The Political Dynamics of European Economic Integration*. Palo Alto, Calif.: Stanford University Press, 1963.
Longo, Michael. *Constitutionalizing Europe: Processes and Practices*. Aldershot: Ashgate, 2006.
Louis, Jean-Victor. "Du projet Spinelli à la Constitution européenne." In *Les principes fondamentaux de la Constitution européenne*. Edited by Christine Kaddous and Andreas Auer. Basel: Helbing & Lichtenhahn, 2006.
———. "Les projets de constitution dans l'histoire de la construction européenne." In *La constitution de l'Europe*. Edited by Paul Magnette. Brussels: Editions de l'Université de Bruxelles, 2000.
———. "La fusion des institutions des Communautés européennes." *Revue du marché commun*, 97 (1966): 843–56.
Lowi, Theodore. "Eurofederalism: What Can European (*sic*) Union Learn from United States?" Pp. 93–117 in *Comparative Federalism: The European Union and the United States in Comparative Perspective*. Edited by Anand Menon and Martin A. Schain. Oxford: Oxford University Press, 2006.
———. *The Personal President: Power Invested Promise Unfulfilled*. Ithaca, N.Y.: Cornell University Press, 1985.
Ludlow, Piers. "From Deadlock to Dynamism: The EC in the 1980s." Pp. 218–32 in *Origins and Evolution of the European Union*. Edited by Desmond Dinan. Oxford: Oxford University Press, 2006.
Lunch, William M. *The Nationalization of American Politics*. Berkeley: University of California Press, 1987.
MacCormick, Neil D. *Liberalism, Nationalism, and Post-Sovereign State*. Pp. 141–55 in *Constitutionalism in Transformation: European and Theoretical Perspectives*. Edited by Richard Bellamy and Dario Castiglione. Oxford: Blackwell, 1996.
Maduro, Miguel P. "Europe and the Constitution: What If This Is as Good as It Gets?" Pp. 74–102 in *Constitutionalism Beyond the State*. Edited by Marlene Wind and Joseph H. H. Weiler. Cambridge: Cambridge University Press, 2003.
Magnette, Paul, and Kalypso Nicolaïdis. "Coping with the Lilliput Syndrome: Large vs. Small Member States in the European Convention." *Politique Européenne* 14 (2004): 1–25.
Mair, Peter. "Political Opposition and the European Union." *Government and Opposition* 42, no. 1 (September 2009): 1–17.
Majone, Giandomenico. *Dilemmas of European Integration. The Ambiguities and Pitfalls of Integration by Stealth*. Oxford: Oxford University Press, 2005.
———. "Two Logics of Delegation: Agency and Fiduciary Relations in EU Governance." *European Union Politics* 2, no. 1 (February 2001): 103–22.
———. "The Regulatory State and Its Legitimacy Problems." *West European Politics* 22, no. 1 (1999): 1–24.
———. "Europe's 'Democratic Deficit': The Question of Standards." *European Law Journal* 4, no. 1 (March 1998): 5–28.
———. *Regulating Europe*. London: Routledge, 1996.

Marquand, David. *A Parliament for Europe*. London: Jonathan Cape, 1979.

McDonald, Forrest. *States' Rights and the Union: Imperium in Imperio, 1776–1876*. Lawrence: University of Kansas Press, 2000.

McKay, David. *Designing Europe: Comparative Lessons from the Federal Experience*. Oxford: Oxford University Press, 2001.

McLaren, Lauren. *Identity, Interests, and Attitudes to European Integration*. Basingstoke: Palgrave, 2006.

Menon, Anand, and Martin A. Schain, eds. *Comparative Federalism: The European Union and the United States in Comparative Perspective*. Oxford: Oxford University Press, 2006.

Mény, Yves, and Claus-Dieter Ehlermann. *A Basic Treaty for the European Union. A Study of the Reorganization of the Treaties*. Florence: Robert Schuman Centre for Advanced Study, 2000.

Mitrany, David. *A Working Peace System: An Argument for the Functional Development of International Organization*. London: Royal Institute of International Affairs, 1943.

Mitterrand, François. *Réflexions sur la politique extérieure de la France*. Paris: Fayard, 1985.

Monti, Mario. "Referendum: *Quid Agendum?* Réflexions pour sortir l'UE de la paralysie assurée." Contribution to the "Etats généraux de l'Europe." Lyon, 20 June 2008.

Moravcsik, Andrew. "Is There a 'Democratic Deficit' in World Politics? A Framework for Analysis." *Government and Opposition* 39, no. 2 (Spring 2004): 336–63.

———. "In Defense of the 'Democratic Deficit': Reassessing the Legitimacy of the European Union." *Journal of Common Market Studies* 40, no. 4 (December 2002): 603–34.

Morgan, Glyn. *The Idea of a European Superstate: Public Justification and European Integration*. Princeton: Princeton University Press, 2005.

Morgenthau, Hans. *Politics Among Nations. The Struggle for Power and Peace*. New York: Alfred Knopf, 1985.

Neustadt, Richard E. *Presidential Power and the Modern Presidents. The Politics of Leadership from Roosevelt to Reagan* (third edition). New York: The Free Press, 1990.

Neville-Jones, Pauline. "The Genscher/Colombo Proposals on European Union." *Common Market Law Review* 20, no. 4 (1983): 657–700.

Nicolaïdis, Kalypso, and Robert Howse, eds. *The Federal Vision: Legitimacy and Levels of Governance in the United States and the European Union*. Oxford: Oxford University Press, 2001.

Norman, Peter. *The Accidental Constitution: The Story of the European Convention*. Brussels: Eurocomment, 2003.

Nuttall, Simon. "Interaction between European Political Cooperation and the European Community." *Yearbook of European Law* 7 (1987): 211–50.

Oddvar, Erik, and John Erik Fossum. "Democracy through Strong Publics in the European Union?" *Journal of Common Market Studies* 40, no. 3 (September 2002): 401–24.

O'Neil, Michael. *The Struggle for the European Constitution: A Past and Future History*. London: Routledge, 2008.

Onuf, Peter, and Nicholas Onuf. *Federal Union, Modern World. The Law of Nations in an Age of Revolutions, 1776–1814*. Madison, WI: Madison House, 1993.

Ostrom, Vincent. *American Federalism. Constituting a Self-Governing Society*. San Francisco: ICS Press, 1991.

———. *The Political Theory of a Compound Republic: Designing the American Experiment*. 2nd ed. Lincoln: University of Nebraska Press, 1987.

Palayret, Jean-Marie. "Visto da Parigi. La Francia, l'Italia e la costruzione europea durante la presidenza di François Mitterrand 1981–1991." Pp. 431–54 in *L'Italia nella Costruzione europea. Un bilancio storico 1957–2007*. Edited by Piero Craveri and Antonio Varsori. Milan: Franco Angeli, 2009.

———. "The French Road to European Monetary Integration during the Maastricht Treaty Negotiations." Pp 242–64 in *Back to Maastricht. Obstacles to Constitutional Reform within the EU Treaty (1991–2007)*. Edited by Stefania Baroncelli, Carlo Spagnolo, and Leila Talani. Cambridge: Cambridge Scholars Publishing, 2008.

———. "Spinelli, entre cellule carbonara et conseiller des princes. Impulsions et limites de la relance européenne dans le projet d'Union politique des années 80." Pp. 355–82 in *Inventer l'Europe. Histoire nouvelle des groupes d'influence et des acteurs de l'Union européenne*. Edited by Gérard Bossuat. Brussels: PIE Peter Lang, 2003.

Parsons, Craig. *A Certain Idea of Europe*. Ithaca, N.Y.: Cornell University Press, 2003.

Pasquinucci, Daniele. *Europeismo e Democrazia : Altiero Spinelli e la sinistra europea 1950–1986*. Bologna: Il Mulino, 2000.

Pierson Paul. "Increasing Returns, Path Dependency, and the Study of Politics." *American Political Science Review* 94, no. 2 (2000): 251–67.

Polsby, Nelson W. *How Congress Evolves: Social Bases of Institutional Change*. Oxford: Oxford University Press, 2004.

Priestley, Julian. *Six Battles That Shaped Europe's Parliament*. London: John Harper Publishing, 2008.

Reh, Christine. "The Lisbon Treaty: De-Constitutionalizing the European Union?" *Journal of Common Market Studies* 47, no. 3 (2009): 625–50.

Rittberger, Berthold, and Frank Schimmelfennig, eds. *The Constitutionalization of the European Union*. London: Routledge, 2007

Rognoni, Cinzia. "Spinelli's Action in the European Parliament: The Crocodile Club, the Institutional Commission, the Draft Treaty." Pp. 286–99 in *The Federal Idea 2*. Edited by Andrea Bosco. London: Lothian Foundation Press, 1992.

Rokkan, Stein. "I voti contano, le risorse decidono." *Rivista Italiana di Scienza Politica* 5 (1975): 167–76.

Sartori, Giovanni. "Constitutionalism: A Preliminary Discussion." *American Political Science Review* 56, no. 4 (December 1962): 853–64.

———. "Concept Misinformation and Comparative Politics." *The American Political Science Review* 64, no. 4 (1970): 1033–41.

Saunier, Georges. "Prélude à la relance de l'Europe: le couple franco-allemand et les projets de relance communautaire vus de l'Hexagone." Pp. 464–85 in *Le couple France-Allemagne et les Institutions européennes*. Edited by Marie-Thérèse Bitsch. Brussels: Bruylant, 2001.

Sbragia, Alberta M. *Debt Wish. Entrepreneurial Cities, U.S. Federalism, and Economic Development*. Pittsburgh: University of Pittsburgh Press, 1996.

Sbragia, Alberta M. et al. "Symposium: The EU and Its 'Constitution.'" *PS: Political Science and Politics* 39, no. 2 (2006): 237–72.

Scharpf, Fritz. *Governing in Europe. Effective and Democratic?* Oxford: Oxford University Press, 1999.

Schmidt, Vivien A. *Democracy in Europe: The EU and National Polities*. Oxford: Oxford University Press, 2006.

Shapiro, Martin. "The Success of Judicial Review and Democracy." Pp. 136–48 in *On Law, Politics, and Judicialization* by Martin Shapiro and Alec Stone Sweet. Oxford: Oxford University Press, 2002.

Sharp, Paul. *Thatcher's Diplomacy: The Revival of British Foreign Policy*. London: Macmillan, 1999.

Shaw, Jo. "What Happens If the Constitutional Treaty Is Not Ratified?" In *The Treaty on a Constitution for Europe: Perspectives After the IGC 2004*. Edited by Ingolf Pernice and Jiri Zemanek. Baden-Baden: NOMOS, 2005. Also online at www.ecln.net/index.php?option=com_content&task=view&id=22&Itemid=40.

Siedentop, Larry. *Democracy in Europe*. London: Allen Lane, 2000.

Smith, Anthony D. *National Identity*. Reno: University of Nevada Press, 1991.

Spinelli, Altiero. *Europa Terza Forza: Politica estera e difesa comune negli anni della guerra fredda. Scritti 1947–1954*. Bologna: Il Mulino, 2000.

———. *Il manifesto di Ventotene*. Bologna: Il Mulino, 1991.

———. "Il modello costituzionale americano e i tentativi di unità europea." Pp. 151–62 in *Il progetto europeo*. Bologna: Il Mulino, 1985.

Stein, Eric. *Thoughts from a Bridge: A Retrospective of Writings on New Europe and American Federalism*. Ann Arbor: University of Michigan Press, 2000.

Steinberg, Richard H. "Judicial Lawmaking at the WTO: Discursive, Constitutional, and Political Constraints." *American Journal of International Law* 98, no. 2 (April 2004): 247–75.

Stetter, Stephan. *EU Foreign and Interior Policies: Cross-Pillar Politics and the Social Construction of Sovereignty*. London: Routledge, 2007.

Stone Sweet, Alec. "The Constitutionalization of the EU: Steps Towards a Supranational Polity." Pp. 45–56 in *Democracy and Federalism in the European Union and the United States. Exploring Post-National Governance*. Edited by Sergio Fabbrini. London: Routledge, 2005.

———. *Governing with Judges: Constitutional Politics in Europe*. Oxford: Oxford University Press, 2000.

Stone Sweet, Alec, Wayne Sandholtz, and Neil Fligstein, eds. *The Institutionalization of Europe*. Oxford: Oxford University Press, 2001.

Stone Sweet, Alec, and James Caporaso. "From Free Trade to Supranational Polity: The European Court and Integration." Pp. 92–133 in *European Integration and Supranational Governance*. Edited by Wayne Sandholtz and Alec Stone Sweet. Oxford: Oxford University Press, 1998.

Storing, Herbert. *The Anti-Federalist: An Abridgement*. Chicago: University of Chicago Press, 1985.

Streit, Manfred E., and Werner Mussler. "The Economic Constitution of the European Community: From 'Rome' to 'Maastricht.'" *European Law Journal* 1, no. 1 (March 1999): 5–30.

Taggart, Paul. "The Domestic Politics of the 2005 French and Dutch Referendums and Their Challenge for the Study of European Integration." *Journal of Common Market Studies*, 44, Supplement 1 (September 2006): 7–25.

Tilly, Charles, ed. *The Formation of National States in Western Europe*. Princeton: Princeton University Press, 1975.

Tosato, Gianluigi. "Simplification of the Treaties as a Constitutional Process." In *Institutional Reforms in the European Union—Memorandum for the Convention*. Rome: EuropEos, 2002.

Walker, Neil. "The EU as a Constitutional Project" Federal Trust Constitutional Online Paper No. 19/04. September 2004. Available at SSRN: http://ssrn.com/abstract=599807 or doi:10.2139/ssrn.599807 (accessed on 27 October 2009).

Weiler, Joseph H. H. "Federalism without Constitutionalism: Europe's Sonderweg." Pp. 54–70 in *The Federal Vision: Legitimacy and Levels of Government in the United States and the European Union*. Edited by Kalypso Nicolaïdis and Robert Howse. Oxford: Oxford University Press, 2001.

———. *The Constitution of Europe*. Cambridge: Cambridge University Press, 1999.

Weiler, Joseph H. H., and Ulrich R. Haltern. "Constitutional or International? The Foundations of the Community Legal Order and the Question of Judicial Kompetenz-Kompetenz." Pp. 331–64 in *The European Courts and National Courts: Doctrine and Jurisprudence*. Edited by Anne-Marie Slaughter, Alec Stone Sweet, and Joseph H. H. Weiler. Oxford: Hart, 1998.

Wiener, Antje. *The Invisible Constitution of Politics: Contested Norms and International Encounters*. Cambridge: Cambridge University Press, 2008.

Zielonka, Jan. *Europe as Empire: The Nature of the Enlarged European Union*. Oxford: Oxford University Press, 2006.

Zürn, Michael. "Democratic Governance Beyond the Nation-State: The EU and Other International Institutions." *European Journal of International Relations* 6, no. 2 (June 2000): 183–221.

Zweifel Thomas D. *Democratic Deficit? Institutions and Regulation in the European Union, Switzerland, and the United States in Comparative Perspective*. Lanham, Md.: Lexington Books, 2002.

Index

About the Contributors

Stefano Bartolini is director of the Robert Schuman Centre for Advanced Studies at the European University Institute. He graduated in political science at the University of Florence and has taught at the Universities of Bologna, Florence, Trieste, Geneva, and the European University Institute. His research interests focus on Western European political development, political parties and electoral history, comparative methodology, and the process of European integration. His most recent books include *The Class Cleavage: The Electoral Mobilization of the European Left 1880–1980* (2000), *Maggioritario finalmente? La transizione elettorale, 1994–2001* (2002), and *Restructuring Europe: Centre Formation, System Building and Political Structuring between the Nation State and the European Union* (2005).

Sergio Fabbrini is director of the School of Government, LUISS University, Rome, and professor of political science at the University of Trento, Italy, and recurrent visiting professor of comparative and international politics at the University of California at Berkeley. He was the editor of the *Italian Journal of Political Science* from 2004 to 2009. He received the 2009 Filippo Burzio Prize for the Political Sciences and the 2006 European Amalfi Prize for the Social Sciences. He has authored eleven academic books, coauthored one book, edited and coedited eleven other books, and published several articles in scholarly journals in the fields of comparative and international politics;

American, European Union, and Italian politics; and political theory. His most recent publications are *America and Its Critics: Virtues and Vices of the Democratic Hyper-power* (2008), *Compound Democracies: Why the United States and Europe Are Becoming Similar* (2007), and, coedited with S. Piattoni, *Italy in the EU: Redefining National Interest in a Compound Polity* (2007).

Andrew Glencross is lecturer in politics at the University of Aberdeen. He previously lectured in the international relations program at the University of Pennsylvania. He holds a BA and MPhil from Cambridge University and a PhD in political science from the European University Institute. His research focuses primarily on European integration, especially in comparison with the U.S. experience of evolving federal arrangements, democratization, and constitutionalism. He has published articles on these topics in the *Journal of Common Market Studies, Political Studies, Government and Opposition, Democratization*, and *European Political Science*. He is also the author of *What Makes the EU Viable? European Integration in the Light of the Antebellum U.S. Experience* (Palgrave, 2009).

Jean-Marie Palayret is director of the historical archives of the European Union, a post he has held since 1991 and associated professor in the history of European integration at the *Institut des Hautes Etudes Européennes* (Robert Schuman University) in Strasbourg. The author of numerous scholarly articles, his books include *L'alliance impossible: diplomatie et outil militaire dans les relations Franco-Italiennes, 1929–1938* (2004), *A University for Europe: Prehistory of the European University Institute in Florence, 1948–1976* (1996) and *Visions, Votes and Vetoes: The Empty Chair Crisis and the Luxembourg Compromise Forty Years On* (2006).

Paolo Ponzano is at present senior fellow at the Robert Schuman Centre of the European University Institute and Chief Advisor of the European Commission. A former collaborator of Altiero Spinelli at the Institute for International Affairs in Rome, he has worked for the European Commission from 1971 to 2009. He was formerly Director of the European Commission for the relations with the Council of Ministers, subsequently for Institutional Matters and Better Regulation. He was also Alternate Member of the European Convention in 2002–2003. He has published about thirty articles in several European journals, including the *Revue du Droit de l'Union Européenne* (Review of European Affairs), as well as a chapter on the institutions of the EU in G. Amato, H. Bribosia, and B. de Witte, eds., *Genesis and Destiny of the European Constitution* (2007).

Alexander H. Trechsel is professor of political science and holds the Swiss Chair on Federalism and Democracy at the European University Institute in Florence, Italy. He was formerly vice-director of the Research and Documentation Centre on Direct Democracy at the University of Geneva, Switzerland. Prof. Trechsel initiated and coordinates the new European Union Democracy Observatory (EUDO) at the Robert Schuman Centre for Advanced Studies of the EUI. He has published articles in *European Union Politics*, the *European Journal of Political Research* and the *Journal of European Public Policy*. He has coauthored a number of volumes, including *The Politics of Switzerland. Continuity and Change in a Consensus-Democracy* (2008), *Towards a Federal Europe?* (2006), *The Future of Democracy in Europe* (2004) as well as the forthcoming title *The Internet Voting Revolution*. His research interests include e-democracy, direct democracy, federalism, European integration, and political behavior.

Bruno de Witte is professor of European law at the European University Institute. Previously he was professor of European community law at the University of Maastricht. He is also codirector of the Academy of European Law and a member of the editorial boards of the *European Law Journal*, *European Constitutional Law Review*, and the *European Journal of International Law*. His main research interest is the constitutional law of the EU, especially its legal structure and the process of treaty revision. His books include *Genesis and Destiny of the European Constitution* (2007), *Ten Reflections on the Constitutional Treaty for Europe* (2003), and *The Many Faces of Differentiation in EU Law* (2001).

Breinigsville, PA USA
12 October 2010
247209BV00003B/4/P